MW00788808

PRAISE FOR
CONSISTENCY SELLING

"Wish I'd been a witness to the brainstorm that caused Weldon Long to write this book. It's simple genius! You can't accidentally produce good results. Effective selling involves implementing a process. Weldon's process is clear cut and has been proven to generate results. I highly recommend that you read this book, then do what he says to do!"

—Tom Hopkins, author of *How to Master the Art of Selling* and *When Buyers Say No*

"As vice president of sales for an organization with a market capitalization of over seven billion dollars, we are always looking for more reliable processes that generate consistent and sustainable sales results. Weldon's principles regarding the sales hallway will help anyone build those powerful results. The information in this book can completely transform your sales outcome if implemented on a consistent basis."

—Gerry D. Heard, vice president of sales,
Service Corporation International

"Over the last thirty years, I have read hundreds of books on sales. Finally, here is a book that demystifies the sales process in everyday language anyone can understand. It will take the reader to the top of the sales ladder! Weldon Long has done it again! Read this book; invest in copies for your sales team, and be prepared to lead the field. Simply profound and profoundly simple!"

—Mark Matteson, best-selling author of *Freedom from Fear* and international sales trainer

"The thing I love most about this book is how the sales strategies are shared—it's not just 'what' you should do but how. The stories and examples of prospect and customer conversations really show you HOW it should sound so you can put the skills into action. Great for anyone in sales from novice to experienced seller wanting to step up their game."

—Andrea Waltz, coauthor of *Go for No! Yes is the Destination, No is How You Get There.*

"F.M. Alexander once wrote, 'People do not decide their futures, they decide their habits and their habits decide their futures.' *Consistency Selling* presents a straightforward, step-by-step sales process that is directly related to sales success. From my experience both as a practicing consulting and clinical psychologist and working in large corporations, success (and failure) is often linked to attitudes and beliefs. *Consistency Selling* addresses the role and necessity of the 'right' mindset to achieve sales success and outlines how to achieve that mindset."

—Ed Nottingham, PhD, author of *It's Not as Bad as It Seems: A Thinking Straight Approach to Happiness* and Consulting & Clinical Psychologist

"Jim Rohn stated, 'The same wind blows on us all. What matters is not the blowing of the wind but the set of the sail.' Never before in our history has the availability of data and information been so readily attainable. While this can be good, that very availability can lead to an intense battle for (and therefore confusion in) the space in the mind of any sales person. Now more than ever, sales people have to be diligent about executing on a repeatable, reliable sales process to stay focused and on task. The absence of one is like being at sea with no ability to navigate; you will end up wherever the waves lead you. *Consistency Selling* prescribes an outstanding solution to the challenge of staying on course. If you want consistent, positive results, you have to read this book."

—Dave Russell, Vice President of Field Sales, a Fortune 100 company

"When I built LightSpeed VT, I knew I had created the most advanced virtual training platform in the world. But I also knew that "nothing happens until something gets sold," so I devoted myself to becoming a sales expert. In *Consistency Selling*, Weldon Long has simplified the selling process by focusing on key behaviors that drive buying decisions. Read this book, implement his simple system, and watch your sales grow faster than ever before."

—Brad Lea, CEO, LightSpeed VT

"I have interviewed thousands of people on my Sirius XM show, but very few have had the impact of Weldon Long. People loved his interview. And the same happened when I put his interview on my podcast. People went crazy— they love Weldon Long! Not only does he have an inspirational personal story, but he offers empowering insights and amazing ideas on building success! This book does the same. It inspires, empowers, and helps you grow your business! Read it, re-read it, and then share it with everyone you know. You will see what I say is true—he is incredible!"

—Dr. Willie Jolley, Hall of Fame speaker, best-selling author of *An Attitude of Excellence* and *A Setback Is a Setup for a Comeback*, and host of *The Willie Jolley Wealthy Ways* show on podcast and Sirius XM Radio.

CONSISTENCY
SELLING

CONSISTENCY SELLING

POWERFUL SALES RESULTS.
EVERY LEAD. EVERY TIME.

WELDON LONG

GREENLEAF
BOOK GROUP PRESS

This publication is designed to provide accurate and authoritative information in regard to the subject matter covered. It is sold with the understanding that the publisher and author are not engaged in rendering legal, accounting, or other professional services. If legal advice or other expert assistance is required, the services of a competent professional should be sought.

Published by Greenleaf Book Group Press
Austin, Texas
www.gbgpress.com

Copyright ©2018 Weldon Long

All rights reserved.

Thank you for purchasing an authorized edition of this book and for complying with copyright law. No part of this book may be reproduced, stored in a retrieval system, or transmitted by any means, electronic, mechanical, photocopying, recording, or otherwise, without written permission from the copyright holder.

Distributed by Greenleaf Book Group

For ordering information or special discounts for bulk purchases, please contact Greenleaf Book Group at PO Box 91869, Austin, TX 78709, 512.891.6100.

Design and composition by Greenleaf Book Group
Cover design by Greenleaf Book Group
Cover images © Kenkuza/ Tiko Aramyan . Used under license from Shutterstock.com

Publisher's Cataloging-in-Publication data is available.

Print ISBN: 978-1-62634-545-4

eBook ISBN: 978-1-62634-546-1

Part of the Tree Neutral® program, which offsets the number of trees consumed in the production and printing of this book by taking proactive steps, such as planting trees in direct proportion to the number of trees used: www.treeneutral.com

TreeNeutral

Printed in the United States of America on acid-free paper

18 19 20 21 22 23   10 9 8 7 6 5 4 3 2 1

First Edition

This book is dedicated to the passionate and hard-working
men and women who eat what they kill in the
sales profession. You are the engines of commerce,
because *nothing* happens until something gets sold.

CONTENTS

FOREWORD

BY STEPHEN M. R. COVEY

Some might think that spending thirteen years in state and federal prison as part of a larger dysfunctional life would be poor qualification for writing a powerful, practical, and inspiring book on sales. But in Weldon Long's case, the exact opposite is true.

Weldon is an extraordinary example of what my father, Dr. Stephen R. Covey, called a "transition person"—someone who choses to stop the transmission of negative tendencies from one generation to another and start passing on those things that tap into the more noble impulses of human nature. In merely five years, Weldon went from being broke, homeless, and a recently released felon to creating a fast growing, Inc. 5000 company with over $20 million in sales and becoming an award-winning author. Both the quality of his life and the contributions he is making today are absolutely remarkable. Before my father's passing, he regarded Weldon as a friend and as one of the finest examples of a transition person he had ever known.

I feel the same. Not only the life Weldon now lives and passes on to his family, but also the concepts he teaches and passes on to society through his work, are ennobling and uplifting. They are also built on solid principles that create both value and trust, which has been my personal area of professional focus for more than thirty years.

With regard to sales, I remember a personal experience I had as a university student years ago, spending a summer selling books door to door. As part of my preparation, I participated in a week of intensive sales training. I learned and practiced sales dialogues, door approaches, and closing techniques. It was like learning a new, unfamiliar language. Some of the techniques never felt right to me. They focused more on how to get potential buyers to do what I wanted them to do rather than what was in their, or their family's, best interest. But Weldon's approach to sales differs by 180 degrees. Both his life and his work are built on many of the solid principles I have discovered through my own work on trust.

For example, I have found that trust is not only a learnable skill, but in most cases, it can actually be restored when lost. It's hard to imagine a better illustration of restoring trust than Weldon. He has exemplified this principle in a very public way by having come from a seriously dysfunctional background to building both a successful heating and cooling business and a tremendous sales training business. In addition, through his writing and thought leadership, he is now helping many others transform their lives and careers.

Weldon's work also reflects the practical application of one of the central messages of my work—that trust is founded on both character and competence. "It's not enough to be good," wrote Henry David Thoreau, "you must be good for something." As Weldon shows, trust is essential to not only success, but also significance in a sales career, where the purpose is to diagnose client needs and recommend solutions that specifically meet those needs. Strong character and great competence are required for building trust and sustainable success in every endeavor— and especially in sales today.

Another central trust message that's reflected in Weldon's work is the critical nature of consistent process. I've discovered that trust is a competency that anyone can develop and get great at through consistent effort and application. Weldon has zeroed in specifically on how this applies to successful selling. As you learn and master Weldon's "Consistency Anchors" and help your customers successfully pass through what he calls the "Sales Hallway," you will greatly increase your ability to find both success and satisfaction in sales.

I'm excited about the journey you have ahead of you as you read Weldon's engaging book and apply its teachings with your prospects and customers. You will find out for yourself that sales is more than just a way to make money; it's a way to make a meaningful contribution and a positive difference in the world. And you will find out how to do that in a way that creates remarkable success and inspires

the kind of trust that builds people, relationships, and confidence in yourself and what you are about.

STEPHEN M. R. COVEY

Author of The New York Times and
1 Wall Street Journal bestseller, The Speed of Trust
Former president and CEO of the Covey Leadership Center

ACKNOWLEDGMENTS

To my wife and children—Taryn, Hunter, and Skylar. Thanks to Mom (for never giving up on me), Susan, Richard, David, and Karen for your love and support. Thanks to Emily Vannelli for making the trains (and bills) run on time, as well as Andy Mitchell and Charlie Pate for all the ideas and creativity. Shout out to Keith Hairston, John Ketchell, and the newest member of our team, Linda Ann Barber.

We all love and miss you, Weeze. Heaven is a lot funnier and better organized these days.

HIGH   HIGH
CHARACTER & Competence = Trust ~ Intro - XV ; p. 17

- • ON A MISSION - P. 10 (Compelling "WHY?") ~ Public Declaration - p. 19
- • CLEAR UNDERSTANDING OF MY JOB - pp. 8,9
- ○ CLEAR, Simple Sales Process - p. 9; 3,4 (vs. Communication skills & ability to wing it) p. 25
- ○ Consistent Activities - pp. 1-3
- ○ Practice & Refine the Process - p. 2
  - ADD & Improve elements

Commission
Sales ≠ making a living = an Opportunity

- ○ Mind Management
  - Cleaning the Brain

CONSISTENT ACTIVITIES PRODUCE CONSISTENT RESULTS

Are your sales sometimes what you want them to be and sometimes not what you were hoping for? Are some months awesome, but other months leave you wondering if you'll be able to pay your mortgage? If so, those are by definition *random* results. And those random results are not coming from consistent sales activities: Those random results are coming from *random* sales activities.

Sporadic and unreliable sales performance usually means you aren't doing the same thing consistently on every sales call. Your actions are random, and as a result, your results are random. It isn't rocket science. It's just a fact of life. Random sales activities will never accidentally start producing consistent sales results. Consistent sales activities will never start producing random results. It just doesn't happen that way in real life. So, as long as your sales activities consist of walking into a call and winging it, your sales results will always be sporadic.

Consistent activities produce consistent results. Random activities produce random results.

THE OPERATIVE WORD IS PROCESS

You never know what is going to be a trigger for your prospect. But if you consistently go through an established sales call process, you will be less likely to miss something that could put you over the top. If you practice and refine your process regularly, you will soon discover practices that are effective with any number of prospects and types of prospects. And as you add each of those practices into your process and repeat them consistently, you'll find your sale performance is improving, because you won't accidentally skip an important part of your process.

One of the most difficult parts of being a professional salesperson is managing the emotional peaks and valleys that accompany the ups and downs of sales. One day you're stoked after closing a huge deal, and the next week you're devastated that you can't seem to close anything. Why is this? What's going on?

Think about it this way: Imagine the operations side of any business. Whether it's engineering, manufacturing, software, banking, insurance, shipping, transportation, service/installation, or telecommunications, think about the quality of the product or service if the operations people were to go about their work in a random fashion.

What exactly would be the quality of the products and services if design, engineering, and technology people just started slapping parts or code together? What if they had no real process, and they just kind of threw things at the wall and hoped they stuck?

What would be the company's reputation for quality? How many customers would be calling to complain about the products or services? How many customers would be calling to accuse the company of misrepresenting the products and services they provide?

Obviously, the quality of the products and services would be very poor. And if you were in charge of operations, you probably wouldn't be employed by that company for very long.

You see, we have an expectation for the operations folks in our businesses to produce quality products and services, and that quality comes from adhering to the process embedded in the operations side of things.

The operative word is *process*. Now, that doesn't mean there isn't an occasional problem. Technology fails. People are human. But as a general rule, following a process to the letter ensures a consistent product and service.

If you want consistently high-quality sales results, the same process applies to the sales profession. If we randomly approach each sales call, we can expect very poor quality in our sales results. If we sometimes do it this way and sometimes do it that way, we are going to produce the same kind of results our operations folks would produce if they went about their work randomly.

CONSISTENT ACTIVITIES
PRODUCE CONSISTENT RESULTS.
RANDOM ACTIVITIES PRODUCE
RANDOM RESULTS.

But here is some really good news: Although a consistent sales process is necessary to deliver consistent sales results, *the process need not be complicated or restrictive.* I don't have any intention of confusing you or putting you in a straitjacket.

JOE THE CONCRETE GUY

In fact, I believe that for the sales process to be effective, it must be simple. If it's overly complicated and restrictive, people won't use it. The confused mind says, "NO!"

And if we don't use the process . . . well, you know the result.

Let me share a story that illustrates a simple yet effective sales process. I learned it from Joe the Concrete Guy.

For many years, I lived west of Colorado Springs, at an elevation of about 9,000 feet in the beautiful little mountain town of Woodland Park, CO. Each morning, I would drive down the twisting canyon of Ute Pass into Colorado Springs. As I drove out of town, I used to pass a quaint breakfast place called The Hungry Bear.

Each time I passed The Hungry Bear, I noticed an old white Ford pickup in the parking lot with bold black letters on the side that read "Joe the Concrete Guy" and a phone number. Seeing that pickup every morning brought a smile to my face as I imagined Joe inside eating his eggs, drinking a cup of coffee, and reading the paper.

For some reason, I enjoyed thinking about Joe like that, and I was envious that he had the time to enjoy a leisurely breakfast with his paper. I wanted to be Joe.

After a couple of years seeing Joe's truck, I was in my yard one day when I realized I needed some steps poured at the end of my driveway to make it easier to access my "writing shed."

A couple days later, I pulled into The Hungry Bear and wrote down Joe's phone number. I was excited to speak with him. I could hardly contain my excitement over getting the chance to meet Joe. We spoke on the phone, and a couple of days later Joe the Concrete Guy was standing in my driveway. I couldn't believe it! Yet I resisted the urge to ask for his autograph.

When Joe got out of his truck, he looked exactly as I imagined—long bushy hair and a long Grizzly Adams beard. He had on shorts, a tee shirt, and flip-flops. There was nothing pretentious or fake about him. He was a real mountain man. In many ways, Joe was like the Honey Badger. If you don't know what I mean, YouTube it.

I stood there in my driveway with this mythical man and explained where I needed the steps. Joe nodded his head and quietly acknowledged that it would be no problem. I asked Joe how much it would cost, and he responded, "Well, that depends on who does it for you."

He continued, "If you don't care about whether or not it starts cracking next spring when the snow melts, I know a guy that'll do it for a few hundred bucks. But if you want me to use my forty years of experience pouring concrete in these mountains so it never cracks, I would have to charge a thousand bucks."

I stood mesmerized by Joe's cool and calm demeanor. "Well, Joe, I don't want it to crack, so I guess it's gonna be a thousand bucks."

Joe smiled like James Dean, and I thought if I had had a cigarette, I would have offered it to him and asked him to smoke it from the corner of his mouth. The dude was beyond cool. Then Joe said, "I appreciate that you understand that I deserve to get paid for what I know—not just for what I do."

My knees nearly buckled.

Just at that moment Joe turned slowly and looked at a motorcycle trailer I had parked in the dirt and rocks next to my driveway. "Why is your trailer sitting there?"

"Well, I mean, you know, that's where I park it, Joe," I timidly responded.

He looked back at me and said, "You park it there on purpose?"

"Yeah?" I was nervously uptalking now, which was a sign of complete uncertainty and subordination to Joe's authority.

"Why do you intentionally park your trailer in the dirt and rocks?" he asked.

I took a giant gulp to assuage the frog in my throat and said, "'Cause the driveway isn't wide enough?" More uptalk.

To which Joe said, "You know, when I'm here pouring your steps, I could widen your driveway."

Realizing I wasn't in trouble with Joe, I exhaled as my budget instantly went from $1,000 to nearly $10,000.

Was Joe pushy? Was Joe doing high-pressure sales? Was Joe selling snake oil?

Of course not. Joe was the consummate sales professional. He identified a problem that I had overlooked and offered a solution. Do you think Joe would have given a damn if I said no to widening the driveway? Do you think his confidence and self-esteem would have been damaged if I said no to widening the driveway?

Not a chance. Joe's confidence in himself and his solutions did not depend one ounce on my approval or appreciation for his work.

Once Joe wrote up the paperwork, I told him, "You know, Joe, I do sales training for a living, and that was a super effective technique to get the ticket higher."

"Technique? What technique?" he inquired.

"Well, that technique you expertly used to get the ticket

7

from $1,000 to $10,000." I was on my turf now, so I was feeling more confident. No more uptalking to Joe.

"Mr. Long, that was no technique. That was just common sense."

"Yes, it was, Joe, but as Voltaire once said, 'Common sense is not so common.'"

Then, Joe went all philosophical on me.

"Mr. Long, take a look at my truck," he instructed. "What does it say on the side of it?"

"Well . . . it says Joe the Concrete Guy and your phone number?" Suddenly I was nervous again at the prospect that I might be in trouble with Joe.

"Exactly." Joe stated. "It says *Joe the Concrete Guy*. Concrete Guy is the main thing, right? I mean it doesn't say Joe the Window, Roofing, Siding, and Concrete Guy. It only says Joe the Concrete Guy."

I stared at Joe in awe, slightly trembling.

"You see," Joe continued, "all I do is concrete. It's all I've ever done since my father taught me how to pour concrete in these mountains. And I learned a long time ago that if I am going to take care of my family, every time I walk onto someone's property, my job is to look for *every* problem concrete can solve and let folks know I can solve it."

Bam. Drop the mic. There is your sales process, people.

You see—Joe's responsibility is our responsibility. When you are with a prospect, your job is to look for every problem your product or service can solve and let folks know you can solve it.

DIAGNOSE PROBLEMS AND RECOMMEND SOLUTIONS

This brings me to the essence of my sales process: Your job is to diagnose problems and recommend solutions. Period. Your customer's job is to buy or not to buy. Period. Your job—diagnose and recommend; your prospect's job—buy or not buy. Say it with me: My job is to diagnose and recommend, and my prospect's job is to buy or not buy!

You'll note that part of my process is to "recommend." That means you must *ask* for the business—sometimes a couple of times. Once you find the problems, you will simply design solutions and use consistency principles to influence your prospect to take actions consistent with buying from you. But more (much, much more) on that later.

. . .

As a general rule, I don't find it very useful to dwell on the past. Whether the memories are good or bad, happy or sad, I find that dwelling on them serves only to distract me from the present moment where real life is happening. And there is usually a lot happening in the present moment.

Nevertheless, I will briefly engage in this indulgence, because it's important to me that you understand that, in order to create real wealth and prosperity in the sales profession, you absolutely must employ a consistent sales process. My story illustrates that point. In my case, developing a consistent sales process transformed my life from one of emptiness and desperation to one of meaning and prosperity.

. . .

In January of 2003, a mere fourteen years prior to this writing, I was living in a halfway house. I was nearly forty years old, and I had nothing. I had no material wealth, no financial security, no job. I had no home, no car, no furniture—nothing.

If you've read my book *The Upside of Fear,* you know that I was in that halfway house because I had just finished twenty-five years of insanity that included desperation, poverty, hopelessness, and thirteen years in state and federal prison. Just your run-of-the-mill dysfunctional life.

Fortunately, by the time I landed in that halfway house, I had experienced a degree of transformation and redemption normally reserved for Hollywood movies. So, by January of 2003, I was a man on a mission to create a life of meaning and significance out of a life where there had been none.

But first I had to figure out how to make a living.

I spent the six months from January 2003 to June 2003 pounding the pavement. I would awaken early each morning, make my bed in the room I shared with six or eight other men, walk to the building next door to get a free breakfast and a sack lunch, and then hop on the city bus in my quest to build my fortune.

Looking back, I must have been a pathetic sight: I was a forty-year-old high-school dropout and a three-time convicted felon who had no resume, no experience, and no job history, stepping off the city bus and knocking on any and every door he could find in a desperate attempt to get a job.

Finding a job and making a living had special significance in my life. I had a ten-year-old son that I had lost seven years earlier when the feds took me away in handcuffs. I was determined to build a successful life and become the father he deserved.

While I had nothing in the way of material wealth or possessions, I did have something that turned out to be of far more value. I was driven to create an honorable and successful life regardless of any obstacles I might face, and I had developed the confidence that I could actually do it. Nothing was going to hold me back. Nothing was going to get in my way. From the isolation of my prison cell, I had learned how to create a Prosperity Mindset.

You can read more about the Prosperity Mindset (and how you can create it) in my book *The Power of Consistency*. A Prosperity Mindset is a powerful and vital complement to the sales process if you are serious about creating wealth and prosperity in your sales career. Having one without the other is like solving only one part of a puzzle. You need all the pieces to successfully put them together. In this book, *Consistency Selling*, I will outline the sales process I developed and combined with the Prosperity Mindset to create unimaginable wealth and success in my life, despite every conceivable obstacle.

And here is the really cool part: Just like me, you can

combine the Prosperity Mindset and my sales process to duplicate my results and create the same unimaginable wealth and success in *your* life. I possess no special skills, talent, or education, and I strongly believe that anything one man can do, another man (or woman) can do.

Okay. Back to my reminiscing.

After six months of pounding the pavement and knocking on doors, I found a job selling air conditioners. I didn't know anything about how air conditioners work (and still don't), but I was lucky to have found any job at that point. I quickly learned that having a commission sales job was not the same thing as making a living—much less creating wealth and prosperity. A sales job gives you the *opportunity* to create wealth and prosperity, but to capitalize on the opportunity, you must have the skills, talents, and processes that will turn the opportunity into money.

I needed money, not just a job. A sales job is no guarantee of income, and you have to be really good at your sales job to prosper over the long term. Otherwise, you end up getting fired or simply walking away, because jobs in sales don't pay unless you can close business.

> IT WAS THE SALES INDUSTRY
> THAT PICKED ME UP, DUSTED ME OFF,
> AND GAVE ME A REAL CHANCE TO
> CREATE A LIFE OF SUCCESS, WEALTH,
> AND HAPPINESS.

Even though I wasn't very experienced in selling, the sales industry immediately changed my life. In my very first month of selling (July 2003), I sold $149,000 worth of air conditioners and earned nearly $14,000 in sales commissions. I was still wearing a Department of Corrections ankle bracelet to track my whereabouts, and I had spent the past seven years making twenty-five to fifty cents per day in prison. That's how fast the Prosperity Mindset and a sales process can change things. It was the sales industry that picked me up, dusted me off, and gave me a real chance to create a life of success, wealth, and happiness.

GOOD WEEKS AND BAD WEEKS

After a couple of months of selling, I quickly learned that despite my high level of motivation (thanks to my Prosperity Mindset), it was very difficult to maintain high levels of sales results. I would have good weeks and bad weeks, but I was unable to maintain any level of sales consistency. While the Prosperity Mindset was an important ally, I needed more. I quickly learned that I also needed a sales process that would deliver powerful sales results on a consistent basis.

I learned a couple of other really important lessons too. I learned that in sales you can spend two hours presenting to a customer, but you only get paid for the last few minutes—depending on whether or not you get a signature. You can spend two hours consulting with your prospect,

13

but if you can't get a prospect to sign on the dotted line, you are nothing more than a brilliant conversationalist and an unpaid consultant. And as Zig Ziglar famously taught us, you are going to have skinny kids.

I learned that, despite looking you dead in the eye, shaking your hand, and promising to call you next Tuesday, prospects often never call back or even remember your name.

I learned that a presentation can go beautifully, but just when you think it's a done deal, prospects will tell you they need to "think about it"—and then never return your phone calls.

I learned that a sale could be within an inch of your grasp, when all of a sudden your prospect needs additional quotes (bids), and the commission you were spending in your head instantly vaporizes into thin air.

I learned that, even if you offer them significantly more value and quality than your competition, your prospects will often compare you to the competition as if you were equals and then demand that you meet the other guy's price. When you can't do that, they go with your cheap competition. It's as if everything you showed them went in one ear and out the other. You feel like Patrick Swayze in *Ghost*. Invisible.

I learned that, once a prospect gets all the information they want from you about your company, your product and services, and your price, they will do and say virtually anything to postpone the pain of making a purchasing decision.

I learned that buyers are not liars; they are simply afraid of getting ripped off like the last time they dealt with a salesperson. Getting ripped off is very painful, and prospects will do anything to avoid the risk and pain of having that happen.

I learned that, if I didn't get really good at dealing with all the excuses, justifications, and postponements that were coming between me and consistent sales results, I was never going to become more than an unpaid consultant. And more important, I was never going to be in a position to get my son back and be the father he deserved.

And guess what? It was actually very easy to get really good at sales really fast. In fact, everything you need to do to build a successful sales career and create real wealth and prosperity in your life is easy. That's the good news. *The bad news is that it will always be a little bit easier not to do it.*

I mean, if you are properly prepared, it's easy to meet with a prospect, take the time to build a relationship based on trust, investigate their problems, design and offer comprehensive, value-based solutions, and formally ask for the order. It's just a little bit easier to drop off a proposal and hope the prospect calls you back next Tuesday.

The problem is Tuesday never comes, does it?

So, for the first six months or so of my sales career, I had a job and made a little bit of money, but I was a million years away from being a professional salesman. I was a million *light years* away from building wealth and prosperity in the sales industry.

I decided to get serious about developing a sales process to complement my Prosperity Mindset. Most of what I knew about sales I had learned by reading the legendary Tom Hopkins while I was still in prison. One of the things Tom talks about is using a sales process to earn the trust of your prospects. Earn their trust, and in many cases, you earn their business. I began to really focus on systematically earning and building trust during my sales process.

EARNING TRUST AND MINIMIZING RISK

Eventually, I figured out that earning trust went a long way toward minimizing the risk prospects often experience during the purchasing process. When you minimize the risk inherent in making a buying decision, you make it easier for your prospects to say yes to you. The higher the risk, the harder it is to say yes. The lower the risk, the easier it becomes to say yes. And when you increase trust, you decrease risk.

As I began to really focus on systematically building trust during my presentations, I began to close more business. It was as simple as that. By focusing on building trust, I was lowering risk and making it easier for my prospects to say yes to me.

Yet it's not enough to be an honest person and depend on your prospect believing you are honest in order to gain trust. As outlined in his bestseller *The Speed of Trust,* Stephen M. R. Covey teaches us that to create real wealth and prosperity in the sales industry, you must engage in specific activities that are designed to communicate high character and high *competence.* You can't leave it up to chance.

When I began to reap big dividends, I came to truly understand the importance of engaging in specific "trust-building" activities with my prospects. It was a critical step on my journey to becoming a true professional in the sales industry. In this book, I will talk a lot about the details of how you will build trust through high character and high competence.

• • •

Things were going fairly well, but what happened next blew the lid off my sales career.

In January 2004, almost a year to the day after I arrived at the halfway house, I was in a bookstore looking for books on selling when I noticed the cover of *Scientific American Mind* as I walked past the magazine rack. I scanned down the cover and noticed a bullet point that read "6 Tricks of Persuasive People."

Since I had achieved real selling success by focusing on minimizing risk and increasing trust, I was not particularly interested in sales "tricks." Tricks were the things that landed me in prison many years earlier, and I had spent a lot of time trying to build a life and sales career based on service, honor, and integrity.

Nonetheless, I flipped through to the article and began to read, and within seconds I was hooked. I couldn't believe the simplicity and power of the words written by Dr. Robert Cialdini. I quickly realized the teaser on the magazine cover was dreadfully inaccurate. Yet here was powerful information that would forever change the level of my success in sales. The teaser should have been "6 Powerful Psychological Realities That Will Help You Crush Your Sales and CHANGE YOUR ZIP CODE"!

CONSISTENCY DRIVES YOUR INCOME

My attention was especially drawn to the principle of consistency. The Consistency Principle stands for the simple proposition that "private declarations dictate future actions," which essentially means that we tend to take actions that are consistent with the things we say to our-selves. I had started the process years earlier of rescripting my habitual thoughts while I was sitting in a prison cell. Changing the conversation I was having in my head had changed everything in my life. I had seen the impact of applying consistency in my personal transformation from being a homeless high-school dropout and convicted felon to a responsible father and productive member of society.

Consistency is the core of the Prosperity Mindset that had fueled my personal transformation and redemption. My private declarations drove different emotions and actions that eventually changed my destiny. Out of a desire to be "consistent" (a desire we all have), I felt obliged to take actions in my life that were aligned with the new things I was saying to myself every day—private declarations dic-tate future actions, right?   (B)

As I read the article, I realized that *public* declarations also dictate future actions. In other words, we are predis-posed to take action on the things we say to ourselves *and* the things we say to *others*.

As you will learn in the process of Consistency Sell-ing, there are certain public declarations, which I refer to as "Consistency Anchors," that are enormously helpful in closing more business.

Like many of us, I had read that if you get prospects to say yes about little things (small concessions), they will often say yes when you ask for the order (big concessions). But this seemed to rely on the prospect mindlessly saying yes out of some kind of subconscious habit. It seemed to depend on trickery and smoke and mirrors.

What Cialdini was saying was different. He was suggesting that people will make logical choices that are consistent with previously declared statements. They weren't saying yes because they had said it by rote twenty times earlier in the sales process. *They would say yes because it made logical and rational sense to take actions that reinforced their previously declared beliefs and convictions.*

I immediately recognized the implications of Dr. Cialdini's research: If I could get my prospects to publicly declare that they didn't need multiple proposals from multiple competitors, that price was not the most important criteria on which they would make a purchasing decision, and that they did not need to "think about it," they would be far more likely to make the purchasing decision in a manner that was consistent with those declarations.

> BUT THEY ARE *MORE LIKELY* TO MAKE A PURCHASING DECISION THAT IS CONSISTENT WITH AND REINFORCES THEIR PREVIOUS DECLARATIONS.

Of course, there are no guarantees. People are free to say that price is not the most important factor in their purchasing decision and then an hour later demand a cheaper price. But they are *more likely* to make a purchasing decision that is consistent with and reinforces their previous declarations. And as I started to design specific consistency activities into my sales process and then combine those with some trust activities I had already developed, my sales career began to come into full bloom.

In fact, I was so confident in my newfound sales process that in late 2004 I opened my own air-conditioning company and used my process to train a powerful sales team. Within sixty months, I grew that company to over $20,000,000 in sales. In 2009, my company was selected by *Inc.* magazine as one of the fastest-growing privately held companies in America.

In 2009, I released *The Upside of Fear,* and I began speaking and teaching full time. I have successfully used my sales process to help thousands of sales professionals simplify the sales process and dramatically increase their sales productivity. In 2013, I released *The Power of Consistency: Prosperity Mindset Training for Sales and Business Professionals.*

As I've stated, the book you are reading is designed to complement the Prosperity Mindset and offer you a step-by-step process to build trust, leverage the principle of consistency, and change your zip code. From small mom-and-pop businesses to Fortune 500 titans in banking, shipping, and insurance, my sales process has proven to be a simple and powerfully effective selling process.

• • •

This book is comprised of two parts. The first section

covers five very important preliminary concepts that are useful to learn and implement Consistency Selling:

Section 1

· Chapter 1: The Prosperity Mindset—Success Is an Inside Job

· Chapter 2: Sales Process versus Sales Result

· Chapter 3: Understanding Market Segmentation—Different Strokes for Different Folks

· Chapter 4: Risk and the Purchasing Decision

· Chapter 5: The Sales Hallway

The second section will walk you step-by-step through the Consistency Selling Process (R.I.S.C.):

Section 2

1. RELATIONSHIP Building

2. INVESTIGATE the Problem

3. SELL Your Company and Your Solutions

4. CONCLUDE the Call

In each step of R.I.S.C., you will learn to do three things:

· You will learn how to accomplish the core activity of that chapter (Build a Relationship, Investigate the Problem, etc.).

· You will learn specific activities to build trust within each step by demonstrating high character, high competence, or both.

· You will learn to ask questions to set "Consistency

Anchors" that you'll use at the end of the sales presentation to earn the prospect's business. Consistency Anchors are public declarations that you'll have your prospect make that will influence their actions at the end of the sales call. For example, you will have your prospect agree with you that price is not the most important consideration and three bids do not ensure making the right purchasing decision. Also, you will have them agree that they can let you know whether or not you are a good fit for them at the conclusion of the process.

You may have noticed that the "C" in R.I.S.C. stands for "Conclude" not "Close." That's because you will never close every sales opportunity, but you can bring every opportunity to a logical conclusion. This is a very important concept in Consistency Selling, because realizing this takes huge levels of stress off you and your prospect.

> "NO" IS A PERFECTLY ACCEPTABLE ANSWER. IT'S THE "I DON'T KNOWS" AND THE "I'LL CALL YOU NEXT TUESDAYS" THAT WILL DESTROY YOUR INCOME-EARNING POTENTIAL.

Listen—in sales, "yes" is best, but "no" is a perfectly acceptable answer. You are going to get some no's in your career, but no won't kill you in sales. It's the "I don't knows" and the "I'll call you next Tuesdays" that will destroy your income-earning potential.

The primary thing I will teach you in *Consistency Selling* is that your main focus on a sales call is simply to get your prospect to make a definitive decision about you and your company *with you sitting in front of them or on the phone*. *Because if you can get your prospect to make a final decision about you and your company with you right in front of them, most of the time that decision will be "yes."*

Prospects don't like to say no directly to you. They like to say no by not returning your phone calls or ignoring your emails. So, if you can nudge them into making a final decision face-to-face or on the phone, the decision will most often be yes.

I am not suggesting that every call will be a one-call close. In many cases, there may be a long sales cycle that includes numerous presentations with various decision makers. What I am saying is that on every sales opportunity there comes a point where it's time to fish or cut bait, and if you go beyond that point, you are playing a fool's game. You will learn to recognize that point in the process and use the tools in *Consistency Selling* to bring the sales opportunity to a logical and reasonable conclusion—one way or the other.

YOU CAN'T JUST WING IT

This is a simple yet incredibly powerful sales process, but before you use it, you must understand the need for a process. Many sales professionals reject the idea of a process altogether, preferring to rely on their communication skills and ability to "wing it."

There is no doubt that strong communication skills are helpful in a sales career, but for some, those skills can serve as a justification for not taking the time to study and master a sales process. And we all know something about human nature: Humans sometimes forget things. When we forget things on a sales call because we have failed to master a process, we can end up skipping one or more key elements that may determine purchasing behavior.

The reality is that we are simply more effective when we have a routine and a process to follow.

Think about the last time you washed your car. Do you typically work systematically around the car, or do you randomly wash a fender here and a window there?

What about a pilot going through preflight procedures? Does she check a little fuel here? A little landing gear there? You'd better hope not.

How about cutting the grass? Do you randomly cut a section here and a section there? Or do you work methodically down the rows of grass? When I cut my lawn, I always start in the same place (right off the front porch) and go clockwise. Then, when I start edging with the Weedwacker, I go counter-clockwise. Because I do it the same way every time, I don't miss any sections, and it consistently looks awesome.

I remember when my son became a teenager and uttered the words I had longed to hear: "Dad, can I cut the grass for some extra money?" After jumping for joy, I showed him how to start the mower, check the oil and gas, and sent him on his way. As he began mowing, I watched horrified from the kitchen window. He was starting in the wrong place! He was starting out by the street! *AND HE WAS GOING THE WRONG WAY!* Immediately, I sprang into action and confronted him out by the street.

"You are starting in the wrong place, son. We start over there—by the porch. And we go the other direction!"

My son looked into my wild eyes like *I was the crazy one* and said, "Dad, are you serious? I can handle this. Just leave me alone and see how it turns out."

Realizing how our exchange must be looking to the neighbors, I walked away with my eyes focused downward and retreated to my secret perch in the kitchen. What I saw was amazing. Despite starting in the wrong spot and going the wrong direction, when he finished, the lawn looked beautiful.

Over the course of that summer, I watched my son as he developed his own process for cutting the lawn. And although his process was different from mine, he did it the same way every time and never missed a single patch of grass.

YOUR PROCESS IS YOUR OWN

The point is this: Your process doesn't have to be the same as everyone else's process, but you must have a process that is comfortable to you and that you use every time. It's the only way to ensure you don't skip an important part of the sales process.

If you are like most of us, you have a process or system for pretty much everything you do, and the reason for that is simple: *Using a process or a system keeps us from missing something.* It keeps us from forgetting to wash a fender, load up with adequate fuel for a flight, or mow a section of the lawn. A process prevents us from skipping an important step in whatever it is we are doing. A process makes us better and more consistent.

Will learning a process take some time? Yes. Is it worth every moment? Yes. It's actually quite easy. The problem is—it's just a little easier *not* to bother.

But I suggest you take the time to study and master the sales process. You don't have to master it overnight, but you will transform you career as you learn the process.

Before we get into the meat and potatoes of *Consistency Selling*, I want you to know that you are capable of building amazing success, wealth, and prosperity in your life and sales career despite any and all past struggles. I am amazed by how life can come full circle.

Recently, I was the keynote speaker at the Colorado Judicial Conference, where I spoke to 400 state court judges. In fact, the judge who introduced me that day was Chief Judge Gilbert Martinez, the very same judge who sentenced me to my final term in prison. That's full circle.

I'm telling you *that* so that I can tell you *this*: There is no challenge you can't overcome. Whether it's a professional or a personal difficulty, you can thrive in the face of adversity if you are willing to create the right mindset and implement the right sales process. Whether it's a bad economy, a cheap competitor, bad leads, or a personal challenge, YOU CAN DO THIS!

PART
ONE

Part One covers some basic concepts that I find are critical to our overall success in sales. First and foremost, I will give you an overview of the Prosperity Mindset, which I believe is critical to having a successful sales career. With a Prosperity Mindset you will conquer the vicissitudes of the sales profession and stay hyper-focused on building your financial dreams. Nothing will hold you back. Nothing will deter you from reaching your true potential.

Then, I will expand on our discussion of sales process versus sales result. You must be able to distinguish between your job and the prospect's job. The process is YOUR job. The result is the PROSPECT'S job. And you must learn not to do the prospect's job for them, lest you find yourself with skinny children.

After that, we will discuss different types of customers and make sure you are focusing on the right ones. You're never going to own 100 percent of your market, so it's important to know who you are and which customers you are pursuing. Yugo dealerships can't afford to give Land Rover service. They shouldn't even try.

I will then discuss the concept of risk in the context of the prospect's decision-making process. Remember: The higher the risk, the harder it is to say yes; the lower the risk, the easier it is to say yes. I will give you specific techniques to systematically lower the risk for your prospects and make it easier for them to say "yes" to you.

Finally, I will discuss the framework of my sales process, which I call the "sales hallway." The sales hallway is a metaphor for the sales process; whether you use my sales process or your company's existing sales process, the sales hallway provides a simple framework through which you will better understand the dynamics and challenges of a sales call.

Let's get started!

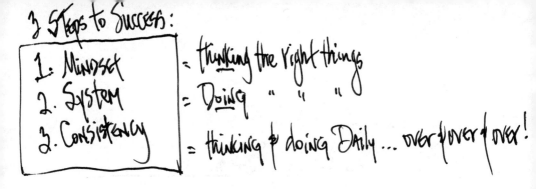

3 Steps to Success:

1. Mindset   = thinking the right things
2. System   = Doing   "   "   "
3. Consistency   = thinking & doing Daily ... over & over & over!

CHAPTER 1

THE PROSPERITY MINDSET—
SUCCESS IS AN INSIDE JOB

I can't stress enough that your sales success and income will be a direct reflection of what you do—not what your customer or your boss or your competitors do.

If you want to create massive and transformational success in your sales career, you need three things: the Prosperity Mindset, the Consistency Selling method, and the consistent implementation of both.

All three are necessary because if you are *thinking* the right things on a sales call and *doing* the right things on a sales call—on a *consistent* basis, you can only create the right sales results.

In this chapter, I will give you an overview of how to create a Prosperity Mindset that will allow you to accomplish anything you want. If you would like a more detailed discussion of the process behind the Prosperity Mindset, I highly recommend that you read my book *The Power of Consistency.*

Of course, there will always be people who will seek to rationalize and justify poor sales performance by blaming forces outside themselves: the economy, the customer, the boss, or the leads. There will always be that guy who says, "I don't understand what's going on. I mean, I'm doing all the right things—but I can't seem to close any business."

That's balderdash. If he were really doing all the right things, over time he would create the right results, because you can't do the right things in sales and accidentally produce the wrong results.

SUCCESS IS AN INSIDE JOB

The first step in creating massive and transformational change in your sales results is acknowledging that you are the responsible party. *Success is an inside job.* That's what the Prosperity Mindset is all about.

I'll illustrate what I mean by the following example. John runs 10 leads and closes 4 of them with an average sale of $5,000 for a total of $20,000 in revenue on his 10 leads. Jane runs 10 leads and closes 5 of them with an average sale of $8,000 for a total of $40,000 in revenue on her 10 leads. Most people would agree that there are sales professionals performing at John's level and at Jane's level.

But would you agree that there are sales professionals performing at John's level and Jane's level in the same town, in the same economy, and with the same customers?

Would you be willing to admit there are sales professionals performing at John's level and Jane's level *in the same company, in the same economy, with the same customers, the same boss, and the same leads?*

Think about this: If you have one person performing at John's level and another performing at Jane's level, and they both face identical external factors, their individual sales results CANNOT be a reflection of external factors. The difference between them relies on INTERNAL factors—and that difference is their MINDSET.

If our sales results were really about the external factors, then all the salespeople in a company facing the same economy and competitors would produce identical sales results. But we know this just isn't true. We know that not everyone creates the same sales results. There are always some folks outperforming other folks in the same company with the same external challenges.

A PROSPERITY MINDSET THRIVES IN ADVERSITY

When I refer to the Prosperity Mindset, I am talking about a mindset that is designed and constructed to thrive in the face of adversity. It's a mindset that prospers in the face of difficulty—in the face of external challenges.

External challenges can never be allowed to determine

your prosperity, because there will always be external challenges. If you are waiting for the external challenges to improve before you create wealth and prosperity, you might as well get comfortable with mediocrity.

What external challenges *can* be allowed to do is determine how hard you are going to have to work to create the wealth and prosperity you want. In other words, if your economy, your boss, and your leads suck, you are going to have to work harder to create success than you would if your economy, boss, and leads are great.

To reiterate: Having a bad economy, a bad boss, or bad leads DOES NOT mean you cannot create wealth and prosperity for your family. It just means you will have to work harder.

• • •

You don't have to be a PhD to understand how to train your brain to do the things you need to do to have the things you want to have. Creating a Prosperity Mindset and programming your brain to make decisions consistent with what you want in your life and career is an easy process. And as I've said before, creating a Prosperity Mindset is easy. It's just a little bit easier to make excuses and *not* do it. The tendency of human nature is to find reasons and excuses to justify not doing the work. It's not uncommon to find many reasons to postpone doing what we know we should do. You need to find just one really good reason to do it.

For example, when my book *The Power of Consistency*

was released in 2013, it hit #5 on *The New York Times* Best-sellers list and #2 on *The Wall Street Journal* Business Bestsellers list. Shortly thereafter, I received a call from a gentleman named Ed Nottingham.

Ed worked for a Fortune 500 company and had devoted his career to teaching executives the relationship between their habitual thoughts, their habitual actions, and their habitual results. In addition to writing a book of his own called *It's Not as Bad as It Seems,* Mr. Nottingham is a PhD and a clinical psychologist.

As we discussed our respective work on the subject of mindset as it relates to success, he said, "You know, Weldon, your book is a very simple explanation of how our neurology affects our choices and the decisions we make. And your explanation of the principles that serve as the underpinnings of Rational Emotive Behavioral Therapy is so easy to understand."

To which I jokingly replied, *"There's a name for this stuff?"*

For me, creating a Prosperity Mindset was just common sense. After all, most of us were taught to "Be careful what you wish for" since childhood, and that little wisdom from Mom is at the heart of creating a Prosperity Mindset.

A PROSPERITY MINDSET IS JUST COMMON SENSE

As we discuss the Prosperity Mindset concept, you will likely think back and recognize times in your life where your thoughts created your results.

We all understand the relationship between success in life and the right mindset. It is very uncommon to see someone with a negative, miserable attitude become successful in sales. Likewise, it is very uncommon to see someone with an ambitious, enthusiastic attitude fail in sales.

Having a Prosperity Mindset is the first step in creating wealth and prosperity in your sales career. When you have a Prosperity Mindset, you have the keys to the kingdom, because nothing will hold you back, and nothing will deter you from achieving your main objectives.

A PROSPERITY MINDSET

- With a Prosperity Mindset, you will rarely get distracted from your key priorities.
- With a Prosperity Mindset, you will succeed, regardless of the external challenges.
- With a Prosperity Mindset, you will thrive in the face of any difficulty.
- With a Prosperity Mindset, you will prosper in the face of any obstacles, whether the obstacle is your economy, your boss, or your leads.

I can't imagine facing my family one day and saying, "We can't go to Disneyland" or "We can't do this or have that," simply because I am unwilling to work harder in the face of external challenges. I couldn't look myself in the mirror. I can't imagine saying, "It's just too hard!"

When the housing market collapsed and took the entire economy with it in 2008, we had just finished our most successful year of sales. Suddenly, my business was hit with the same economic challenges facing every business in the country.

What amazed me was how many companies in my industry and other industries were closing their doors and facing real financial collapse. My Prosperity Mindset would never allow the external economy to determine my destiny, so I decided we were going to have to reorganize and work harder just to hang on to what we had worked so hard to achieve.

And that's what we did. I was fine with working twice as hard and getting twice as good at sales to just tread water. It beat the hell out of the alternative, which was to turn tail and run. As a result of the general climate at the time, our business dipped in 2008 and 2009. But because of our reorganization, cost cutting, and increased focus on selling, we continued to thrive.

Remember: You simply cannot allow external factors to determine your success.

Let's get into the process of creating a Prosperity Mindset.

SMALL DECISIONS DETERMINE YOUR DESTINY

The following statement might seem contrary to logic, but it's true: The first step in creating a Prosperity Mindset is understanding that success requires making the right decisions in the *seemingly inconsequential moments* of your life.

> IT'S THE SMALL AND SEEMINGLY INCONSEQUENTIAL DECISIONS WE MAKE A MILLION TIMES OVER THE COURSE OF OUR LIVES THAT DETERMINE OUR DESTINY.

Most of us operate under the misconception that our life is a reflection of the big moments of our lives. But in reality, it's the small and seemingly inconsequential decisions we make a million times over the course of our lives that determine our destiny.

When you have a big decision to make, you will usually think about the decision consciously, debate your options, and come up with what you think is the best decision. Because you put so much thought into the decision, it's usually the right decision.

But a problem arises when we make small, seemingly inconsequential decisions *without consciously thinking about them.*

Consider this: You leave your work to drive home. On the way, you are listening to music, drinking a cup of coffee, and navigating traffic, all the while never missing a turn or hitting another car. During the trip, you might even take a phone call from a customer or your kid and carry on a conversation—still never missing a turn or hitting another car. Suddenly, without ever *consciously* thinking about the directions, you pull into the driveway of your house.

Somehow you navigated all the turns and twists in the road (the seemingly inconsequential events) automatically, without a conscious thought.

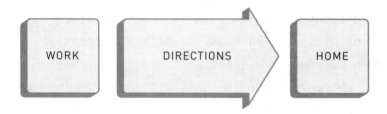

We've all had that experience, right? It's amazing that we can navigate a 2,000-pound automobile along twists and turns in the road and hundreds or even thousands of other cars, without even a conscious thought about where we're going.

But ask yourself this simple question: Could you have driven to that same house without *consciously* thinking about it the very first time you went there? Of course not. You would have needed a map, GPS, or a realtor to help you get there.

Nevertheless, once you made the trip from your work to your home several times, eventually the directions to your house went from your conscious mind to your subconscious mind. When something becomes a subconscious activity, we call it second nature. And when something becomes second nature, we can do it without a deliberate, conscious thought.

We humans refer to the route between our work and our home as "directions," and the individual twists and turns have no significance in and of themselves. They are by definition *seemingly inconsequential events.* In other words, if I were in a helicopter and saw your car turn from Main Street onto Elm Street on your way home, there would be no significance to what I saw—it's just a car turning from one road onto another road. The individual components of the directions mean nothing.

Nevertheless, if you string those seemingly inconsequential twists and turns together in the same order every time, how often do you reach your desired destination? That's right: every time. You can't follow those directions and accidentally end up across town in the wrong location. If you follow the directions the same way every time, you will reach your destination every time.

If you can relate to the experience of driving home without consciously thinking about where you're going, you can apply the same principle to going from wherever you are in your sales career to wherever you want to be in your career.

The key is making the correct seemingly inconsequential decisions every time, because if you do, success is guaranteed. You can only fail to reach your destination if you fail to make the right seemingly inconsequential decisions every time.

For example, suppose you are currently making $50,000 per year—that's your current location—and you would like to go to a new destination of $200,000 per year. Are there certain things you would need to do to reach that new destination? Of course there are! And those things are called the directions, and those directions are the seemingly inconsequential decisions you make in every sales opportunity. When you make the correct seemingly inconsequential decisions about how you run the sales call, you will end up at the desired location.

You can't follow the directions to $200,000 per year and accidentally end up at $50,000 per year. You can't *do* the right things and *accidentally* produce the wrong results.

Now, keep in mind that at first you will need to concentrate on the directions to $200,000 per year, just like you had to concentrate on the directions to your house the first time you drove there.

But if you continue to follow the directions, eventually the directions will go from your conscious mind to your subconscious mind, and the seemingly inconsequential things you need to do to reach your desired destination will become second nature.

So the key is simply figuring out where you are ($50,000), where you want to go ($200,000), and what you need to do to get there. Once you figure that out, it's a very simple process to take the directions from your conscious mind to your subconscious mind and begin automatically doing the things you need to do to reach your desired destination.

In this book, I am going to give you the step-by-step directions to get to a prosperous sales career.

Here is a concept I discuss in *The Power of Consistency*.

Imagine you have a box in front of you right now, and in that box are all the parts you need to build a beautiful motorcycle. Everything you need to build the motorcycle, including step-by-step instructions, is in the box—there are no extra parts and no missing parts.

Now imagine that you accurately follow all the instructions, and piece by piece and part by part you begin assembling the components that are in the box. You put the handlebars where the handlebars go; you put the engine where the engine goes, etc. At some point, you look down, and the box is empty. You have followed the instructions and properly assembled all the components.

What is the likelihood that when you step back to admire this beautiful mechanical creation you have built, you realize that instead of building a motorcycle, you have accidentally baked a cake?

Not very likely, is it? You can't focus on following the instructions to build the motorcycle with the motorcycle components and accidentally bake a cake. The universe and the laws of physics simply don't work that way.

The box is a metaphor for your mind; whatever is in your mind is all that you can build. Your thoughts are the instructions, and your expectations are the components of your life and business.

Piece by piece and part by part, your life comes out of your box in the form of your decisions, which are a reflection of your habitual thoughts and expectations. Every time you make a choice, you are reaching into your box and making a *seemingly inconsequential decision* and pulling a little piece of your life and business out of your box.

At some point, you will be at the end of your sales career, and you will have removed all of the contents of the box as you make a multitude of seemingly inconsequential decisions.

You can only remove from the box those things that are in it. You don't accidentally create your sales results any more than you can accidentally bake a cake out of motorcycle parts. Your sales results are the reflection of the contents of your box and the instructions you are following.

Therefore, the results in your sales career are simply a reflection of the instructions you are following to assemble what's already in your mind. Ask yourself if you ever experience thoughts or expectations like these:

· Customers just want a cheap price.

· Customers don't care about our service, value, and quality.

· Customers don't want to hear my spiel.

· Customers just want to know how much it costs.

· Customers always go with the cheapest company.

· Customers won't change suppliers unless we're cheaper.

· Customers always have to get three bids.

· Customers always have to "think about it."

· Our prices are too high.

· These leads suck.

· Cold calling is a waste of time.

· I'm too good for cold calling.

· I'm never going to make enough money to buy that new house.

· I'm never going to make enough money to send my kid to private school.

· I'm never going to make enough money to buy my spouse that new car.

· Salespeople are snake oil peddlers, and I am better than them.

· People who make a lot of money in sales are high pressure, and I am better than them too.

· I am also morally superior to salespeople.

· I can't wait until I get a *real* job so I can quit this sales job!

If any or many of those thoughts and beliefs make up the contents of your box, what do you suppose you are going to pull out of it? What seemingly inconsequential decisions might you be making regarding your sales activities on a daily basis without giving them a conscious thought? What impact might those seemingly inconsequential decisions have on your sales results?

GARBAGE IN, GARBAGE OUT

It always amazes me the degree to which some people will go to rationalize poor sales performance. If you have thoughts like the ones listed previously, you shouldn't be surprised if you are not pulling wealth, prosperity, and powerful sales results out of your box. If you have thoughts and expectations like the ones listed previously, that's all you will be able to create in your sales career.

It's just like the old computer adage—garbage in, garbage out.

Let me give you an example of how our thoughts and expectations impact our results.

Recently, I was speaking with a young man who owns a plumbing company. His dad had owned the company for twenty-five years, and now he (the son) had taken it over.

As we spoke, the young man complained endlessly about the economy and cheap competitors in the plumbing industry, and he bemoaned the fact that he could not make any money. His business was struggling.

Finally, at one point in the conversation, he said to me, "Ya know, it's like my dad always said—plumbers don't drive Cadillacs."

I thought to myself, "There's your sign, buddy."

The funny thing was, a couple of weeks later, I was in Tampa Bay, Florida, for two days working with the sales team at one of the most successful plumbing companies in the country. After day one of the training, the owner, Scott Vigue, invited me out to his house for dinner and to check out his new boat.

Just as I pulled in the driveway, his wife was backing out of the garage. What do you suppose she was driving? That's right—a Cadillac Escalade. I thought to myself, *Hmm. I guess some plumbers do drive Cadillacs.*

We got into the Escalade and drove to a marina, where we walked out to see his new boat. That boat turned out to be a 65-foot, *3.5 million dollar yacht!* I thought to myself, *Hmm. I guess some plumbers drive Cadillacs and yachts.*

So on one hand, you have plumbers who don't own Cadillacs, and on the other, you have plumbers who own Cadillacs and yachts.

The question is, which man is right? And of course the answer is both of them are right. Both men are the products of their thoughts and expectations. Both men are reflections of whatever is in their boxes—for better or for worse. In *The Power of Consistency,* I discuss why those thoughts and expectations that you have in your head about sales eventually leave your head and create the reality in your sales results.

I will remind you that I am no PhD, psychologist, or neuroscientist, so my discussion of these concepts is very basic. With all due apologies to Dr. Ed Nottingham, Dr. Albert Ellis, and others, this is just my explanation of why the things in your box (thoughts and expectations about sales) eventually come out to create your reality (sales results). Four words explain why your beliefs and expectations about sales create your sales results.

FOUR WORDS WILL INFLUENCE YOUR RESULTS

- Thoughts
- Emotions
- Actions
- Results

When you have a thought, a signal is created in your brain that chemically creates a corresponding emotion. The emotion drives you to take some action or another, which generates a corresponding result. Therefore, your emotions and actions (which create your results) are a reflection of your thoughts.

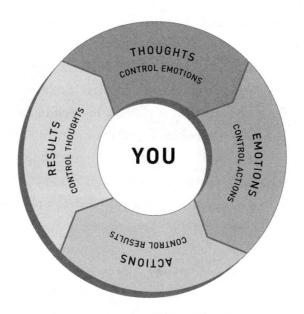

(It is true, as Tony Robbins teaches, that you can change your physical "state" and that will also change your emotions. However, for purposes of this discussion we are focusing on how your *thoughts* about sales influence your *emotions and actions* with respect to your sales calls.)

For example, if you have a fearful thought, your brain will create a fearful emotion. You will *feel* frightened. If you have a warm and loving thought, your brain will create a warm and loving emotion. You will *feel* warm and loving.

Once you feel the emotion, you will act in a manner consistent with your emotion. Once you take an action, you will create a result that is a direct result of the action. It's like falling dominoes. The thought comes first; then, the emotion, action, and result follow.

For example, suppose your kid runs out in the street. You immediately have a fearful *thought* that your kid could get seriously injured or killed. Instantaneously, you have a fearful *emotion* and the adrenaline kicks in, which drives you to take *action* to go into the street and rescue your child. The *result* is that your child is safe. Congratulate yourself on some excellent parenting.

This process repeats itself countless times over the course of your day. You have a thought that triggers an emotion that drives an action that creates a result. Now, here is where things get a little tricky. As it turns out, your emotions and actions (which create your results) are a reflection of your thoughts—*even if your thought is wrong or inaccurate.*

In other words, you can experience a very real emotion, take a very real action, and create a very real result *based on a thought that is wrong or inaccurate.* We call this a self-fulfilling prophecy, and it's why your mother said, "Be careful what you wish for."

It also explains why your thoughts and expectations about sales eventually create your sales results—even if your thoughts and expectations are wrong.

• • •

Here's another scenario: Imagine you're walking down a dark street with your family, and a very menacing-looking character approaches you. In one hand, he has a gun; in the other, he has a knife. He is covered in blood and rushes toward your family in an obvious attempt to hurt or kill someone.

Immediately, you have a panicked and fearful thought. You know you must protect your family in the face of this threat.

The thought instantly triggers a corresponding emotion, and as the adrenaline courses through your body, you spring to life like a super hero, charging the assailant. With a swift uppercut, you connect with his jaw, knocking him off his feet. He lands on the back of his head and is rendered unconscious. The result? You have protected your family from a dangerous situation.

So far so good, right? Not so fast, Rocky.

When the police arrive and the assailant regains consciousness, you learn that he was no threat to you or your family whatsoever. Your thought was inaccurate. You misinterpreted the situation. It turns out the gun was fake. The knife was fake. The blood was fake. The person you assaulted was harmless. He was on his way to a Halloween party.

Does the fact that your thought was wrong change the way you *felt* and *acted* when you *thought* he was a threat? Even though the thought was not real, how real were the emotions you felt? How real were the actions you took? How real is the result of the guy's broken jaw?

As the police handcuff you for assaulting an innocent man and load you in the back of a patrol car, you watch your family fade into the distance and think to yourself, *Wow. How could I have been so wrong?*

It's easy to understand when you realize that your emotions, actions, and results can be the product of irrational, incorrect, and even self-destructive thoughts. And despite the *false nature* of the thought, the emotions, actions, and results that flow from it are *very real.*

Once you understand that wrong or inaccurate thoughts can drive very real emotions, actions, and results, you are on the precipice of an exciting new understanding of how wealth and success can be created in your sales career.

Consider a sales professional whose basic thoughts are: *People don't care about my company's service, quality, and value. They just want a cheap price.* What would be the very natural *and real* emotions that would emanate from those thoughts? No doubt, they would be emotions of defeat and surrender and inevitable failure.

And then—what would be the logical actions that would come from those emotions? Would that emotion generate an action of delivering a powerful and dynamic sales presentation designed to convey the service, quality, and value of his company? Of course not! The only action that is consistent with his thought and emotion would be delivering a half-hearted effort while dropping off the cheapest price possible.

And what would be the results of those actions? The salesperson leaves the sales opportunity dejected and commission-less while mumbling to himself, "I knew it. I knew these prospects don't care about our quality or service!"

Our friend has become the quintessential self-fulfilling prophecy. His wrong, inaccurate, and self-destructive thoughts have created very real and impoverished emotions, actions, and results. He blames his misery and pathetic sales and financial results on his leads, his boss, his customer, or the economy. He doesn't see the connection between his thoughts and expectations and his results. In his mind he is a victim of circumstance. It's a pretty safe bet he will have a different job very soon—whether he wants it or not.

A BETTER PERSPECTIVE

Now let's take a look at another sales professional. His basic thoughts look like this: *I get it. Money is tight for my customers. But they want my company. They need my company's service, quality, and value. Now, more than ever, people need my company, and it's my job to demonstrate the value of my company. And if I do my job, customers will pay me a few thousand dollars extra because they want quality and service.*

What are the emotions that will emanate from those thoughts? Emotions of invincibility, emotions of inevitable success, and the feeling that he is ten-feet tall and bullet-proof. And what actions flow from those emotions? The sales professional engages in a dynamic and compelling sales presentation that is designed to communicate the service, quality, and value of his company.

Not surprisingly, the results are amazing: The

customer says yes to high value and high-quality solutions at a premium price. The customer is willing to pay for the confidence and trust he feels in the sales professional.

And our Sales Super Hero says the same thing as the lonesome loser: "I knew it. I knew these prospects care about our quality and service!" Both men are products of their thoughts and expectations. The man who believes he will succeed is right. The man who believes he will fail is likewise right.

Albert Einstein once said, "We cannot solve our problems with the same level of thinking that created them." I'll go a step further and say, *"You cannot change your sales results at the same level of thinking that created your sales results."*

If you want to change your sales results, you must first change your thoughts and expectations about your sales and your customers.

If you want to temporarily change your sales results, focus on your actions. If you want to permanently change your sales results, focus on your thoughts.

THE UPSIDE OF FEAR

If you understand the relationship between your thoughts and expectations and your sales results, you may want to follow a simple yet powerful process to change the contents of your box. I base the process on the acronym of FEAR, which stands for Focus, Emotional Commitment, Action, and Responsibility. It will help you accomplish two things.

First, the process will allow you to take an inventory of your box and replace any "junk in your trunk" with the things in your life and business you really want. This process will help you identify what you want in your sales career and place those things inside your box. Once your sales objectives are placed inside your box, you will eventually reach back in, pull them out, and begin making seemingly inconsequential decisions consistent with the things you want.

Second, the process will show you how to program your subconscious mind to follow the directions to where you want to go in your sales career. You will program your subconscious mind to follow the directions to your desired destination (income) in the same way you drive home from work without consciously focusing on the directions.

The process will take some effort and a little time, but success is totally within your grasp. Remember that you had to focus and concentrate on the directions to your house the first few times you drove there, but eventually the directions were programmed into your subconscious mind and became second nature. In the same way, you will initially need to focus and concentrate on the directions to your new income and sales goals, but eventually those directions will also become programmed into your subconscious mind and become second nature.

So let's get started on identifying what you really want to achieve in your sales career and the directions you'll need to follow to get there.

FEAR: FOCUS

The first step in the FEAR process is to get *focused* on your sales and income goals and the directions you need to follow to reach them. The things you identify in this step will provide the raw materials for a specific plan that you'll put together in the next step.

First, you must specifically identify your sales and income goals.

You can express these goals in many ways, but the best way is whatever feels most natural and meaningful to you. The important thing is that you are very specific and precise in identifying them.

In his classic book, *Think and Grow Rich,* Napoleon Hill identified a series of characteristics possessed by the world's most successful people. Interestingly, he identified two of those characteristics on the first page of the book, and the first one was having a "definiteness of purpose." In other words, *focus.*

Successful people have a specific and *definite* objective. They aren't milling about aimlessly hoping they hit something. They have a specific target. So however you decide to express your sales and income goals, the only requirement is that you are specific and definite.

You might identify your income goal as earning $200,000 per year, or you might express it as retiring at sixty with $2,000,000 in your retirement account. It doesn't matter how you express it, so long as it's specific. In other words, you would not want to express your income goal as a generic "getting rich" or being "successful."

You might express your sales goal as selling $10,000,000 per year or being the #1 producer in your company. Either way is fine as long as you have a specific way to measure it. You will know whether or not you sell $10,000,000 per year or whether or not you are #1 in your company. Keep in mind that in sales "what gets measured gets done." It is critical to have specific income and sales goals so you can identify exactly when you achieve them.

In the first company I built, just eighteen months after walking out of a halfway house, I set my sales goal as "achieving and maintaining a #1 market share position." By monitoring permits issued by the county, I would easily be able to monitor my progress.

Within our second year, we achieved the #1 market share position and never released our hold on it. In fact, over the last four years I owned that company, we were issued *twice* as many permits as our nearest competitor and many times more than the other companies who fought over our scraps.

Second, you must identify only two or three things you need to do to reach your goals.

These two or three things will serve as the directions you will follow and will program to become second nature later in this process.

Now you may be thinking, *There are way more than two or three things I'll need to do to achieve my income and sales goals.* That may be true. But what is important here is that you identify only the *most important* things you need to do.

> WHAT IS IMPORTANT HERE IS THAT YOU IDENTIFY ONLY THE *MOST IMPORTANT* THINGS YOU NEED TO DO.

You've no doubt heard of the Pareto principle that stands for the proposition that "80 percent of your results come from 20 percent of your activities," and this is especially true in sales. While there are a lot of things that will make you successful, you must identify the "leveraged" activities that generate results. When you stay FOCUSED and execute on those activities like a champ, the little things will fall into place and take care of themselves.

For example, one of my clients in the insurance industry figured out that if he and his sales team each made five new cold calls per day, everything else would take care of itself. And he was right. Over the past several years, his agency consistently reached its sales and revenue goals. He just keeps everyone focused on one simple goal: making five new cold calls per day.

Now, does he also engage in sales and mindset training to improve sales productivity? Absolutely! But his singular *focus* each day is to ensure that he and his team each make five new cold calls per day—and everything else seems to take care of itself.

There are three activities (directions) that you need to focus on to successfully sell on a consistent basis. I define directions as the things you need to do consistently to reach your sales goals. You may use any or all of these activities— in addition to any you discover that might be specifically relevant to your sales success. The important thing is to institute *consistency* into everything you do.

FOCUS ON: PASSION, DIAGNOSING AND RECOMMENDING, AND ASKING FOR THE ORDER

· Run every call with passion and purpose.
· Diagnose every problem and recommend solutions on a consistent basis.
· Ask for the order every time.

You will understand each of these directions in detail after you complete *Consistency Selling*, but in the meantime, it's vital to identify only a few key leveraged activities that will create the income and sales results you desire, and then stick with them.

Once you've identified your income and sales goals and the two or three things you need to do on a consistent basis to reach them, you have the raw materials to put together a simple plan to achieve them. I call this a Prosperity Plan.

The next step in the FEAR process is Emotional Commitment. In this step you will put your income and sales goals into your box and program the directions to reach them to become second nature.

FEAR: EMOTIONAL COMMITMENT

I mentioned earlier that Napoleon Hill identified only two characteristics of the most successful people on the first page of *Think and Grow Rich*. The second of those is a "burning desire" to achieve the definite purpose.

A burning desire requires a deep emotional commitment to the income and sales goals you listed in the Focus step. It's not enough to have only a passing desire to achieve these goals.

An emotional commitment means making your income and sales goals *and the things you need to do to achieve them* (the directions) another strand of your DNA. They must invade every cell of your body.

Getting emotionally committed requires three simple steps and the creation of a Prosperity Plan.

CREATING YOUR PROSPERITY PLAN

· Write down your goals and the things you need to do to achieve them in the present tense as if you have already achieved them.
· Review your goals for 10 to 15 minutes per day in a daily Quiet-Time Ritual,
· Allow yourself to experience the emotions of achieving your income and sales goals as if you have already achieved them. This is important, because as you'll recall your emotions, actions, and results are a reflection of your thoughts—*even if the thoughts don't actually reflect reality.*

Remember, your thoughts become a self-fulfilling prophecy, so the goal here is to create more positive thoughts to trigger more positive emotions, actions, and results.

When you write out your income and sales goals and the directions you need to follow to achieve them in your Prosperity Plan, it might look something like this:

I earn $200,000 per year.

1. I run every call with passion and purpose!

2. I diagnose problems and recommend solutions like a BOSS!

3. I ask for TRUST every time!

I generate $2,000,000 in annual sales.

1. I make 5 new cold calls EVERY DAY!

2. I am responsible! I am powerful! I am awesome!

Remember that you can write out your income and sales goals and the directions to achieve them in whatever format or way feels comfortable for you. These may be different depending on your industry or goals. You can use my example or create your own. What matters most is that the income and sales goals and the things you personally need to do to reach them are *specific*.

For example, if you set an income goal, specify the amount: "I earn $200,000 per year," or "I have $1,000,000 saved by my 60th birthday." If it's a sales goal, you could write: "I sell $2,000,000 this year," or "I sell 500 units this month."

Now, ask yourself a simple question: If you followed the directions you wrote out, what is the likelihood you would reach your income and sales goals? It's probably very high, because you simply cannot do the right things and accidentally create the wrong results. You can't follow the directions to $200,000 and accidentally end up at $50,000 any more than you can follow the directions to your house and accidentally end up across town.

We will discuss how to ensure you follow those directions in the Action step next, but first we must program the directions to your income and sales goals into your subconscious mind so that you begin to do them on a second nature basis. We do this by engaging in what I call a Quiet-Time Ritual.

A QUIET-TIME RITUAL

A Quiet-Time Ritual is simply taking 10 to 15 minutes per day and reviewing your Prosperity Plan. As you review your income and sales goals and the directions you have outlined to achieve them, allow yourself to imagine what it will feel like when you have reached your goals. Allow yourself to emotionally experience the achievements. As Napoleon Hill once wrote, "Imagine yourself already in possession of them."

As you review your Prosperity Plan each day, you are placing the goals you want to achieve and the things you need to do to achieve them inside your box. Then, throughout your day, you are reaching into the box and pulling out *seemingly inconsequential* decisions that are consistent with the things you want.

Remember, Napoleon Hill said we need to have a "burning desire" to achieve our "definite purpose." Through this daily Quiet-Time Ritual, you will get deeply emotionally committed to the income and sales goals on which you are now focused.

Once you do that, you will see how you start taking action *automatically* toward your new income and sales destination in the same way you drive home from work without thinking about the directions. It all becomes second nature.[1]

FEAR: ACTION

At the end of the day, action is what separates the winners from the whiners. The really great news is that if you discipline yourself to write out your Prosperity Plan and review it daily in your Quiet-Time Ritual, you will find that you automatically start taking action that will get you to your desired income and sales destination. Once you begin taking action, the results are pretty much guaranteed. Taking action consistent with your Prosperity Plan is the result of

---

[1] For a more detailed and comprehensive explanation of the Prosperity Mindset, the Prosperity Plan, the Quiet-Time Ritual, and how you can create transformational results in ALL areas of your life, I strongly recommend that you read *The Power of Consistency*.

your Quiet-Time Ritual because of a little thing called cognitive dissonance.

Cognitive dissonance is a huge driver of human behavior, and it can be easily understood as the anxiety you feel when you don't do something you said you would do, or the uncomfortable feeling of holding two competing thoughts. In other words, if you were to tell me that you would pick me up at the mall at 3:00 p.m. and then realize at 3:15 p.m. that you forgot to pick me up, the anxiety you feel is called cognitive dissonance. And when you feel it, it drives you to take some action. You would either call me or hurry to the mall or do something, but you would not just ignore the feeling and forget about me standing in front of the mall with no ride.

Human beings do not like being in a state of cognitive dissonance, so when we feel it, we are driven to take action to get rid of it. And the way we do that is to do the thing we said we would do or rationalize that we never really needed to do it in the first place.

For example, if you tell yourself you are going to lose ten pounds and then a few hours later you find your face buried in a tub of ice cream, you will feel cognitive dissonance. To get rid of the dissonance, you will either stop eating the ice cream or tell yourself you never really needed to lose ten pounds in the first place. In either case, the dissonance will decrease, and you will feel better—but only one of those actions will help you reach your goal of losing ten pounds!

So with that as a backdrop, imagine the following

scenario: You awaken early, and as you have your morning coffee, you pull out your Prosperity Plan and enjoy your Quiet-Time Ritual. For ten to fifteen minutes, you review your income and sales goals and visualize yourself doing the things you know you need to do to reach them. You allow yourself to bask in the glow of financial success. You allow yourself to experience the emotion of being a true sales professional and realizing your true income potential. You revel in it. You allow yourself to feel the "burning desire" of achieving your "definite purpose." You imagine yourself already in possession of it.

Now, imagine it's a few hours later, and you have your first sales opportunity of the day. But instead of running the call with passion and purpose, diagnosing problems and recommending solutions like a professional, and then asking for the order, you casually go through the motions and drop off a cheap proposal without ever formally asking for the order.

What do you suppose you are going to feel? Exactly! You are going to feel cognitive dissonance, and you are going to feel like crawling out of your skin, because only hours earlier you painted a much different picture of how you were going to run your sales calls. *Remember, private declarations dictate future actions!*

You are going to want to shed the cognitive dissonance like a cheap suit, because it doesn't feel good to lie to yourself. So to get rid of it, you will have a choice: You can either start running your sales calls the way you know you should, or you can tell yourself you never really needed to earn $200,000 a year in the first place. In either case, the dissonance will decrease and you will feel better, but only one of those actions will help you reach your income and sales goals.

You see, the Prosperity Plan and Quiet-Time Ritual are the ultimate in personal responsibility. The Consistency Principle stands for the basic proposition that "Private declarations dictate future actions." So if you tell yourself you are going to do something, you either have to do the thing or rationalize to yourself that you never really needed to do it in the first place. Either way will let you off the hook and let you feel better, but only one of those ways will change your life.

If you stay consistent with the Quiet-Time Ritual, you will very quickly start doing the things you know you need to do to reach your income and sales goals. There will be no place to run and no place to hide. It's the only way you'll be able to look yourself in the mirror or your family in the eyes. And before you know it, you will be following the directions to your income and sales goals without even thinking about it consciously. The actions will become second nature in the same way you drive to your home without a conscious thought.

Writing out your Prosperity Plan and engaging in a daily Quiet-Time Ritual is easy, and it will drive transformational income and sales results for you and your family. That's the good news. The bad news is that it will always be just a little bit easier not to do it. Only you can decide if you want the results badly enough to remain committed to consistency.

FEAR: RESPONSIBILITY

The final step in the FEAR process is Responsibility. Specifically, this means understanding that your life is a reflection of your choices, and your choices are your responsibility and your responsibility alone.

Listen, everyone has difficulty and challenges in sales. Everyone has problems in sales. Everyone faces prospects who want multiple bids and a cheaper price. Everyone has prospects who want to needlessly postpone the purchasing decision by saying they need to think about it.

The highest-paid sales professionals are not earning a lot because they somehow avoid these challenges. They face the same sales challenges we all face, but they thrive and prosper in the face of those challenges—not in the absence of them.

You can have a very difficult problem in sales, but your ultimate results will not be a reflection of the problem; they will be a result of the *decision* you make about the problem. Better decisions guarantee better results.

And when you face that problem, you have to make a decision about how you are going to respond to it. And where do you suppose your decisions are going to come from? That's right—they come from your box. You will reach in your box and pull out a decision every time you face a problem, so you'd better know what's in that box. And it'd better be something you put in your box during your Quiet-Time Ritual—not something that got in there without your permission.

When you change your thoughts about sales, you change your emotions. When you change your emotions about sales, you change your actions. And when you change your actions in sales, you change your results.

Before you know it, you are looking at homes in a new zip code!

Now that you have the basics of how to create a Prosperity Mindset, you are prepared to learn a powerfully effective sales process. But first, there are a few sales concepts I need to explain.

First and foremost, we will discuss the necessity of focusing on your sales *process* rather than the sales *result*. It's very common for sales professionals to prejudge what they believe the result will be, and if they anticipate a bad result, they often abandon the process—which, of course, guarantees the bad result.

Next, we will review different types of customers and focus on creating value for the customers who value us. We don't want everyone as a customer.

Then, we will review the impact that risk has on the purchasing decision and how to diminish risk for our customers. As noted earlier: The higher the risk, the more difficult it is for prospects to say yes to us. The lower the risk, the easier it is for them to say yes to us.

And finally, we will review the "sales hallway." The sales hallway is a framework I use to explain the sales process and the challenges you face as you navigate the sales hallway with your prospect.

Once you understand these basic concepts, you will be prepared to learn and implement a simple yet powerfully effective Consistency Selling process.

Let's do this!

CHAPTER 2

SALES PROCESS VERSUS SALES RESULT

In sales, you have two key components: the sales *process* and the sales *result*. The sales process is everything you do (build a relationship, identify problems, solve problems, and ask for the order), and the sales result is everything the prospect does (buy or not buy).

You have 100 percent control over how well you do your job, and you have 0 percent control over how well the prospect does their job. Yes, you can *influence* your prospect (the better you do your job, the more likely a prospect is to say yes to you), but at the end of day, the prospect makes the ultimate decision about whether or not they are going to give you their money in exchange for your solutions to their problems.

STAY FOCUSED ON HOW AWESOME YOU ARE

One of my strongest recommendations is that you stay focused on how well you do your job. In other words, you have 100 percent control over how awesome you are. You have 100 percent control over how well prepared and skilled and confident you are on any given sales call. So it only makes sense to stay focused on those areas over which you have control.

Many sales professionals focus way too much energy on the sales result (the prospect's job) over which they have no control. This is a very stressful way to sell, because you are basing the measurement of your success on something someone else controls.

My measurement of success is based on how well I do *my* job, not on how well the prospect does *his*. In other words, if I do an awesome job running my sales call—I am well prepared, highly trained, and top-notch at serving my customer—but the prospect chooses not to buy from me, does that mean I have failed? If I base my measure of success only on my close rate, then the answer is yes. If I base my measure of success on how well I built the relationship, diagnosed the problems, solved the problems, and asked for the sale, then the answer is no.

Keep this in mind: If you are executing your sales responsibilities at a high level, the numbers will follow. You may do a great job *on an individual sales call* and still not get the order. On other occasions, I can do a lousy job and get the deal. Am I a success if I do a lousy job on a sales call and accidentally stumble into a sale? Not in my book. You have to base your measurement of success on what *you* do—not on what your prospect does. Otherwise, you will develop a false sense of your performance.

It's when you have long periods of bad sales results that you need to take a look within.

> MY JOB IS TO DIAGNOSE
> AND RECOMMEND;
> THE PROSPECT'S JOB IS TO
> BUY OR NOT TO BUY.

That's why it is so important to stay focused on what you do (diagnose problems and recommend solutions) and let the prospect do their job (buy or not buy). Tell yourself: "My job is to diagnose and recommend; the prospect's job is to buy or not to buy."

Stay focused on what you can control. Winners obsess on improving what they control (the process), and whiners obsess on what they can't control (the result). Be a winner, not a whiner.

And finally—keep in mind that following a sales process is not about high pressure. It's about high service. The more you stay focused on diagnosing problems and finding solutions for your customers, the more you will generate sales through high service.

- WINNERS = obsess about what they CAN control (THE Process)
- WHINERS = " " " " CAN'T control (THE Result)

* HIGH Pressure vs. HIGH Service! *

SIMPLER IS BETTER

Maybe it's because I'm a very simple guy with an IQ of 103, but I love simple, straightforward things—the simpler the better. The great thing about simple things is that they are easy to learn and, therefore, easy to use.

Most any sales process will produce positive results if it is used correctly. The problem is that if a process is too complicated, it won't be used. Our confused mind will just say no. And when that happens, we abandon the process and end up relying on pushy sales tactics or a cheap price to close business.

Let's face it: During a sales call, things can happen that can knock you off your beam. An important call comes in that the prospect has to take. The prospect's assistant comes in with an urgent matter. An important meeting has suddenly been called. There is no end to the obstacles that can come up. But if you have a process, you'll stay on track. Focus on your process of identifying and solving problems, and the results will take care of themselves.

I was once closing a training opportunity worth about a hundred grand. The prospect got a call during the presentation announcing that the sales training budget had been suspended for the current quarter. Imagine handling that objection! Talk about a mood killer. Yet I simply stayed focused on my process, and offered the client an option to do the training now and be billed the following quarter. Bingo! So much for that smoke screen, right? People will come up with a million reasons to say no. Our job is to find just one reason for them to say yes!

FOCUS ON THE PROCESS

Oftentimes, a salesperson will prejudge the opportunity and decide the prospect can't afford this or wouldn't want that or that they are going to go with a cheaper competitor. When that happens, the tendency is to abandon the sales process, as the salesperson has already decided what the result is going to be. Of course, this becomes a self-fulfilling prophecy.

Recently, I was on an in-home sales call with a salesman who works for a client of mine in Orange County, California. When the salesman and I greeted the homeowner, her first words were, "Just so you know, you are the first of three companies I have coming out to give me a price. I am a purchasing agent for a hospital and I ALWAYS get three bids."

Upon learning that we had a professional buyer on our hands, it would have been very easy to abandon the process and just focus on getting the price as low as possible. That was especially the case here, because my client is a premium-quality and service company and they simply do not compete on price. They are never going to be the cheapest solution, but they offer outstanding service and quality. As a result, the owner, Leland Smith, has grown annual sales to over $50,000,000.

"a premium-quality & service company... we simply do not compete on price"

"3 Bids"

Despite the prospect's proclamation about three bids, I confronted the "three-bid myth" head-on during the sales presentation. I asked her, "Ma'am, have you ever known anyone who got three bids for a project for their home and ended up choosing the wrong company?"

"I am sure it happens," she responded.

I continued, "Have you ever had a bad experience with a contractor in your home?"

"No. I've been very fortunate, but it's because I do my due diligence."

I could see she wasn't going to concede anything. She was a very sharp lady, and she did not want to give me any ammunition. Yet I persisted. I'm pretty sharp, too.

"I must tell you, ma'am, you are one of the luckiest people I've ever met. Almost everyone I've ever met has had problems with contractors in their home. You should play the lottery," I said through a wry smile.

She smiled a little but said nothing, but I was not going to give up. After all, this was a *training* sales call, and I had one of my client's top salesmen with me. I wasn't going to get punk'd in front of him.

So I forged on. "Ma'am, are you kidding with me? I mean you have *never* had a problem with a contractor?"

She stared at me for a few seconds and then I smelled blood in the water when she said, "Well, there was the one time with the guy who remodeled my bathrooms." She glanced at her husband. I knew I was making big progress.

"What happened?" I asked.

"It ended up taking twice as long as it was supposed to, and the change orders ended up doubling the price. I wasn't very happy."

It was time for me to go for the kill. "How did you find him?"

Slowly she said, "I talked to a few friends about who they used, then did my research and met with several companies." She smiled at me and said, "I guess that's your point, isn't it?"

I immediately asked her the key question. "Ma'am, if on one hand you had three bids from three companies who could say anything to get your money, and on the other hand you had our company, who would guarantee you high quality and a 'no change order' guarantee, which of those would you prefer?"

"I see what you're saying," she responded.

"Does that mean you would prefer our company?" I asked.

"Yes."

I knew in that moment I had the deal. And about an hour later we walked out with the order for a premium job at a premium margin.

My point is you cannot afford to prejudge the result and abandon the process. The process delivers consistent results even when things don't seem ideal. Focus on the process. Let the results take care of themselves.

SELLING ON SOMEONE ELSE'S TURF

The distractions are even more frequent and bizarre if you are selling on someone else's turf. Whether it's windows, siding, life insurance, health insurance, mortgages, air conditioners, furnaces, carpet, remodeling, groceries, roofing, vacuum cleaners, or textbooks, selling on someone else's turf takes a special breed of human being.

Things happen on a prospect's turf that do not happen in our office where we control the environment. Sometimes the prospect's wife will announce, "Dinner is ready!" just as you are entering your closing sequence. Sometimes the kids need some homework help at a crucial point in the sales process. Sometimes little Johnny needs Daddy's attention. Sometimes the dog relieves himself on your shoe.

Whatever the distraction, it's critical to have a process, and that process must be simple. But do not mistake simplicity for weakness. I once read a Steve Jobs interview where he credited "focus and simplicity" for his success. If it was good enough for Jobs, it's good enough for me.

THE CONSISTENCY SELLING METHOD

The Consistency Selling process follows four simple steps (R.I.S.C.). In each step, you will learn specific trust-building activities and seven "Power Questions" to close the escape-route doors and set Consistency Anchors.

THE FOUR STEPS OF
CONSISTENCY SELLING—R.I.S.C.

Step One: Build a RELATIONSHIP.

Building a good relationship with your prospect is vital to building trust. During this step, you will learn simple ways to build trust by demonstrating **high character.**

You will also learn how to use the first Power Question to close the "**multiple bid/proposal**" escape route. You will set a **Consistency Anchor** to get your prospect to acknowledge that multiple bids and proposals are not always the best way to ensure a good purchasing decision.

Step Two: INVESTIGATE the problems.

In sales, we are compensated based on the number of the problems we can solve for our customers. The more thorough our investigation is of a prospect's problems, the more likely we are to be in a position to offer multiple solutions. During this step, you will learn simple ways to build trust by demonstrating **high competence.**

You will also learn how to use the second Power Question to close the "I want to think about it" escape route. You will set a **Consistency Anchor** to get your prospect to acknowledge that they can make a final decision about you and your company, with you in front of them, at an agreed-upon time.

Step Three: SELL your company and your solutions.
Once you have built a relationship and thoroughly investigated your prospect's problems, you will demonstrate why your company's products and services are the best options for them. During this step you will learn simple ways to build trust by demonstrating both high CHARACTER and high COMPETENCE.

You will also learn how to use Power Questions #3, #4, #5, and #6 to slam the price door shut. You will set numerous **Consistency Anchors** to get your prospect to acknowledge that price is not the most important criteria on which they will base their purchasing decision. They will also acknowledge that cheap providers usually cut their prices by cutting quality and that they do not want you to cut your price by cutting quality.

Step Four: CONCLUDE the sales call.
Remember the "C" here is for "Conclusion," not "Close." You cannot close every sales call. No one has a 100 percent conversion rate, and if you do, you need to dramatically increase your prices, because you are giving away the farm. During this step, you will learn how to leverage the trust and consistency anchors to bring the sales opportunity to a conclusion.

> You will also learn how to use Power Question #7 to ask for the order in a very simple yet powerful way: "Mr. Prospect, the only question I have for you now is simple. Will you trust me with these recommendations?"

As you go through the four steps, you will engage in specific activities to build trust through high character and high competency and ask seven Power Questions that are designed to have your prospect make certain public declarations that ultimately lead to the prospect taking actions consistent with purchasing from you. Each question is set up with a specific conversation designed to get the public declarations you need. Here is a list of the seven Power Questions:

1. (After sharing your company's guarantees and a powerful signature story about something amazing you've done for a previous customer.) Mr. Prospect, if on one hand you had three proposals from three companies that might tell you anything to get your business, and on the other hand you had one company like mine that would guarantee the results you want and would treat you the way we treat our customers, which of those companies would you prefer?

2. (After sharing an article from an industry trade magazine or expert that states price is not the most important factor when purchasing whatever it is you sell.) Mr.

Prospect, would you agree or disagree with this industry expert report that there are several factors as important, perhaps even more important, than a cheap price?

3. Mr. Prospect, have you ever had a bad experience with a pushy salesperson? Well, I am not that person. I am a professional, and I won't be the person calling you all next week bugging you about this purchase. What I have found is best for my customers is to take all the time I need to answer all your questions, make sure I design the right solutions, and get those solutions within your budget. All I ask is that you let me know one way or the other whether or not I'm a good fit for you. And "no" is a perfectly acceptable answer. Does that sound fair enough?

4. (After completing a demonstration showing how your product and/or service is superior, ask Power Questions #4, #5, and #6 in succession.) Mr. Prospect, when you consider how important these factors are to ensuring the superior quality of our products and services, why do you suppose other providers cut corners when it comes to the quality of their products and services?

5. Mr. Prospect, if a company cuts those corners at the expense of quality, have they really saved you any time and/or money?

6. Mr. Prospect, later we are going to look at some solutions and some investment options. Sometimes

when people see how much the best-quality products/ services cost, they want to know if I can lower the price. Now that you understand the corners we would need to cut to lower the price, is that something you're going to want me to do?

7. (At the very end of your presentation.) Mr. Prospect, the only question I have for you now is simple. Will you trust me with these recommendations?

> WHAT WILL DESTROY YOUR ABILITY TO EARN A SIGNIFICANT INCOME IS ACCEPTING "I DON'T KNOW" AND "I'LL CALL YOU BACK NEXT WEEK."

Remember, you can bring every call to a logical conclusion—either yes or no. And I'll say it again. While "Yes" is best, "No" is a perfectly acceptable answer. A "no" will not kill you in sales. You will get plenty of them in your career. What will destroy your ability to earn a significant income is accepting "I don't know" and "I'll call you back next week." Your responsibility is to bring the sales call to a reasonable conclusion at the appropriate time.

We all know there comes a time in a sales opportunity to fish or cut bait. Maybe it's a one-call close or maybe it's a six- or twelve-month sales cycle, but at some point, our gut tells us when we are getting strung out. And when you learn to bring the call to a conclusion at the appropriate time—yes or no—you will dramatically improve your sales performance and keep your dignity and self-respect.

> YOUR RESPONSIBILITY IS TO BRING
> THE SALES CALL TO A REASONABLE
> CONCLUSION AT THE APPROPRIATE TIME.

Focusing on your process rather than focusing on the outcome of the call will remove stress from your sales day and your sales career. When you are obsessing on what someone beyond your control is going to do (buying or not buying), you'll feel uncertainty and anxiety—like riding in a car with someone who is driving too fast in heavy traffic. The feeling of being out of control can cause heart palpitations.

On the other hand, when you concentrate on your process, you will end up feeling calm, confident, and in control. If you feel any uncertainty at all, it will be because of your own lack of preparation and training. But you can quickly fix that by learning and mastering the Mindset and Consistency Sales principles in this book.

When you focus on your sales process, you will be the master of your sales destiny.

CHAPTER 3

UNDERSTANDING MARKET SEGMENTATION—DIFFERENT STROKES FOR DIFFERENT FOLKS

It's important to remember that in sales, no one thing will work 100 percent of the time. Succeeding in sales is all about doing the very best you can on every call. However, there is a certain element of variability that enters into the equation. It's very helpful to understand that in each sales opportunity, there are different strokes for different folks. In other words, there are many different types of customers, and each group has different priorities.

In the broadest terms, I separate customers into three distinct categories, or what I like to call "Market Thirds," composed of the Value Third, the Cheap Third, and the Undecided Third. Visually, it might look like the following figure.

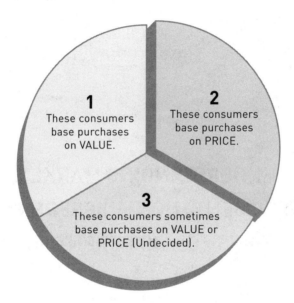

Let's discuss each group.

The Value Third customers are the ones we all love. They value the value. They value quality and service, and obviously, they are great customers. A member of the Value Third expects high service and quality, and they are willing to pay for it. They don't like cheap, and they don't buy cheap. In most cases, these folks are nice. They are the type of person that, even if there is a problem with a product or service, they will be reasonable about it. They are unlikely to bite your head off at the first sign of a problem.

Being in the Value Third does not mean the customer

is rich. I have met many value-based customers who have average incomes, but they still buy quality. In many cases, they will postpone the purchase until they can afford to buy high quality.

Then, we have the Cheap Third. The customer in this group cares about one thing and one thing only: price. They don't care about quality. They don't care about service. They don't care about anything except getting a cheap price. They don't care if you are in business next year to service your products. In some cases, they don't even seem to care about the safety of their families.

I remember back when I owned a residential heating and air-conditioning company in southern Colorado, and I was on a sales call where the homeowner kept hounding me about giving him a cheaper price. As I always did, I shared with him the components of a quality installation and demonstrated some of the corners my less expensive competitors often cut to save time and money.

As we discussed the issues of quality, service, and proper installation to protect his investment and his family, he continued to hammer me on a cheap price.

> YOU CAN'T FIX STUPID. AND YOU CAN'T
> MAKE SOMEONE CARE ABOUT SOMETHING
> THEY DON'T CARE ABOUT.

Finally, I showed him a highly publicized ABC News

story that reported how an entire family lost their lives in a $9,000,000 home in Aspen, Colorado, as the result of what appeared to be the faulty venting of a high-efficiency furnace.[2] The alleged improper installation resulted in a fatal carbon monoxide leak, which led to the deaths of the prominent Denver couple and their two small children. I explained that going cheap is rarely the best option when you are dealing with the complicated installation of gas appliances.

He gazed at me, still unconcerned, and said, "Your company is going to be too expensive for my taste."

My point is simple: You can't fix stupid. And you can't make someone care about something they don't care about. You are always going to come across customers who will base their buying decision on the sole factor of a cheap price. The bottom line is that each group is very different. Nevertheless, as different as the Value Third and the Cheap Third are, they do have one thing in common: Both groups will ask you for a discount at some point during your sales presentation.

That's right, even the Value Third will most likely ask for a price concession at some point, but here is the thing: *The Value Third will still buy from you even if you don't drop the price IF you are able to show them why you cannot drop the price.*

It goes without saying that the Cheap Third will not buy from you *unless* you drop the price. You have to make sure

2   http://abcnews.go.com/US/story?id=6376209&page=1.

that the price objection is really a price objection. After all, you might have a Value customer just testing the pricing waters out of habit and will buy from you whether or not you drop the price.

If you give a price reduction too quickly, you end up giving valuable margin away to the Value Third customer that you didn't have to give, and you give a discount to the Cheap Third customer who will only ask for more discounts when they smell blood. Let me give you an example that demonstrates how quickly some sales people go to the discount option—even when it's unnecessary.

THAT SOUNDS A LITTLE STEEP

Several years ago, I was traveling from the southern-most part of Colorado back to my hometown of Colorado Springs. I had been speaking to a group of prisoners at the Federal Correctional Complex in Florence, Colorado, and one of my staff was traveling with me.

As I made the hour-long drive, we heard on the radio that we were expecting our first winter storm of the year, so I was in a hurry to get home.

As I made my way north, my son called me from college. "Hey, Dad, there is a storm coming, and I need to get snow tires on my car." It was his first semester away at school, so it was important to me that he got the right tires on his car. I told him to go to a tire store and call me from there.

A little while later, he called and handed his phone to a sales guy in the tire store. "Hi, sir," the salesman said. "I've got your son here, and he seems to need some snow tires."

"That's right," I responded, "but I need to know you can get the tires on tonight. There is a storm coming, and I don't want him out driving in it with old tires."

To which the salesman relied, "That is not a problem, sir, we have twenty customers waiting in line for new snow tires, and no one is leaving here tonight without them. We'll stay till midnight it we have to."

Well, that was exactly the service and attitude I was looking for, so I was sold. I am, after all, a Value Third customer, largely because I didn't have anything till I was forty years old. And because I work hard for my money, I hate buying cheap things that don't last. Moreover, we were talking about snow tires for my son—probably not the best time for me to go cheap.

"Sounds great," I told the salesman over the phone. "What are my options?"

"Well, we have your basic cheap snow tires, your mid-range snow tires, and your Mack Daddy Awesome snow tires."

Since I am in the Value Third, and it is my son whom I value dearly, I said, "Give me the best snow tires you've got. How much are they?"

After a few moments on his calculator, he comes back on the phone and gives me a price around a thousand bucks.

I told him to hold on while I reached for my wallet to

retrieve my credit card. Just as I was about to read him the credit card number, the staff member sitting next to me said, "Ask him for a discount."

"Excuse me?" I said. "I am not in the mood to negotiate. I just want some snow tires for my kid and to get home."

"Just ask him and see what he says."

So instead of reading the salesman my credit card number, I turned back to the phone and said, "Dude, that sounds a little steep."

That is all I said: "Dude, that sounds a little steep."

Then, without as much as uttering a syllable, I hear the salesman on his calculator crunching numbers.

In a moment, he comes back on the line and says, "How about I knock $200 bucks off? Does that sound better?"

Really? I couldn't believe my ears. I wasn't even serious! On a gag, this guy knocks $200 off a set of snow tires!

Now, I don't know a lot about the tire business, but I am guessing that on a $1,000 set of snow tires, there is about $500 to $600 worth of gross margin, and this guy just gave away 40 percent of the gross margin to me because I said, "Dude, that sounds a little steep!"

What do you suppose I would have said to the guy if he'd said to me, "I understand it sounds like a lot, but these are my best snow tires, and we do have about twenty customers waiting ahead of this snowstorm—I mean, if you want to call back in the summer to discuss a discount, that's fine, but I can't do any better than that tonight."

I would have started reeling off "4837 . . . " After all, I still had my credit card in my hand!

To understand the total stupidity of what he did, you must remember, he gave me 40 percent of the gross margin on a set of SNOW TIRES in a BLIZZARD! With twenty cars deep in line!

The moral of the story is that you never know initially if a price objection is a real price objection or is just being raised out of habit, or on a lark, or, in my case, as a joke. If you automatically drop the price to get the deal, you will give away precious margin to Value Third customers when it isn't necessary. And if you give the discount to the Cheap Third customers, they will only ask for more. If you sell like this, you are going to have skinny kids.

HOLDING YOUR GROUND

When we get into the closing strategies at the end of this book, you will learn that you have to hold your ground when it comes to price objections. You have to probe a little to determine whether it's a legitimate price objection or just a fishing expedition. If it's a real objection, you'll find that out in due time and you will need to be prepared to deal with it.

I remember a few years ago I was buying a new SUV. I test-drove the car, made the deal, and was sitting in the salesman's office as he wrote up the purchase agreement. As he was doing his paperwork, I got up to walk around the showroom and noticed a gorgeous Jaguar XKR convertible with 510 supercharged horsepower. When I was a kid, I always thought Jags were the most exotic cars on the road. The car was unbelievably beautiful.

As I walked around the car admiring it, the salesman came out of his office and asked, "You want to take one of these home today too?"

"Not today, Jim. My limit is one car per visit, but maybe next time."

As we talked, I walked around the front of the car and noticed a tag hanging from the rearview mirror that read, "zero percent financing for 36 months."

"Jim," I inquired, "I can get zero percent financing on this car?"

To which he smiled and said, "You want one now?"

Of course, I said, "Yes!" We went back into his office to do the paperwork on the Jag.

As Jim wrote up the buyer's order, he got down to the bottom of the page where he wrote in the purchase amount. He wrote down the MSRP right off the sticker price.

"Jim, what are you doing?" I asked.

"I am writing up the paperwork."

"Jimmy, Jimmy, Jimmy," I responded. "You've got to give me a significant discount on the Jag. After all, I have purchased several cars from you over the years. Hell, I am buying two cars from you today!"

Jim looked me dead in the eye without ever missing a

beat and said, "Weldon, I can give you the 0 percent financing or I can give you a discount, but I can't do both."

To which I responded . . . "OK."

You see, you can say no to a price concession with a value-based customer like me, and we will stay still say, "Yes!"

Suppose Jim had said, "OK, I'll knock a couple grand off the sticker price."

In that case, he would have sacrificed $2000 of gross margins AND his 25 percent of the gross margin, which is $500 in additional commission—that he didn't need to sacrifice!

When someone asks you for a price concession, hold your ground, probe a little bit, and find out if it's really necessary to close the deal. If your customer turns out to be a value-based customer, you'll save yourself margin and commission. If your customer turns out to be a cheap customer, you're probably already screwed, and dropping your price will only lead to more demand for price concessions.

NOT ALL PROSPECTS ARE CREATED EQUAL

Now, let's talk about the Undecided Third. This group often vacillates between the Value Third and Cheap Third. Sometimes they will go Value, and other times they will go Cheap. It just depends on the product or service, and sometimes it just depends on their mood or on the relationship with the salesperson.

There are a lot of folks like this out there. They drive

their Mercedes-Benz to Walmart. But they are good customers, because they are actually trying to decide if they should go Value or Cheap on a particular purchase, so they will *listen* to you. And these folks are very susceptible to coming over to the Value Third if you do your job and demonstrate why this purchase is an important time for them to go Value.

So suppose you position yourself and everything you do in order to appeal to the value-based customers and try to get as many of those undecided customers as you can. Then suppose you are successful in influencing HALF of the Undecided Third. How much of the pie do you have? *Exactly!* You have 50 percent of the pie, and you have the fat, juicy, high-margin half of the pie—not the nasty, crusty, no-fruit-filling part of the pie!

You can build a very lucrative sales career on half of the pie IF you go after and successfully earn the business of the correct half of the pie. So never forget that not all prospects are created equal. Not every customer makes the purchasing decision based on price alone. You've got to remember there are different strokes for different folks. Remember this conversation about market thirds.

CHAPTER 4

RISK AND THE
PURCHASING DECISION

When consumers decide to purchase something, they have a lot of questions. They have questions about quality, warranties, the company, and—of course—the price. But what they are really trying to evaluate is the amount of risk they might incur by making the wrong purchasing decision. Remember: The higher the risk, the more difficult it becomes for them to say yes; the lower the risk, the easier.

One of the ways to earn more business and sell at better margins is *to minimize risk* for your prospects. I will show you three simple ways to consistently and systematically minimize risk for your prospects and therefore make it easier for them to say yes.

Imagine you go to Walmart to buy a flashlight. You

stand in front of the flashlight shelf and pick one up. You go through the checkout counter, pay, and go home with your new flashlight. But when you get home, you realize you just don't like the way the flashlight works or feels in your hand.

What do you do? Most likely you return the flashlight to Walmart. And what happens when you take it back to the store? They give you a new one, or they give you your money back—right? So how much risk did you take in making your original purchasing decision? None. Zero. If you don't like it, you return it, so there is no risk of making the wrong purchasing decision.

Imagine this scenario: You're standing in front of the flashlight shelf, but instead of that flashlight costing $15, it cost $150. And on the bottom of the shelf is a sign that reads ALL SALES FINAL. NO REFUNDS. NO EXCHANGES.

Did it just get riskier to buy that flashlight? Did it just become more difficult to make a purchasing decision? Of course it did, because the risk of making the wrong purchasing decision just became significantly higher. Now, ask yourself this question: As you debate whether or not to buy the $150 flashlight with no possibility for refunds or exchanges, what options begin going through your mind?

You think, *Hmm, maybe I better go see what The Home Depot and Costco have for flashlights. Maybe I need to see if I can get a lower price. Oh, I just don't know! Maybe I should take some time to think about this. Maybe I don't even need a flashlight!*

Sound familiar? It should, because the high risk of

making the wrong purchasing decision drives consumer behaviors that can make your sales career frustrating and difficult. A high level of risk will cause prospects to say the things that you deal with every day. Perceived high risk makes people start thinking:

I want to think about it.
I want a cheaper price.
I want more bids/proposals.

For decades, retailers have minimized risk by offering liberal return policies. If a consumer is standing in the aisle contemplating the purchase of a new flashlight, they are more likely to buy it when they know if they get home and don't like it, they can return it. When there is no risk of making the wrong purchasing decision, it's easier to say yes.

DYSFUNCTIONAL BUYING BEHAVIOR

Imagine you are going to spend a significant portion of your hard-earned money on insurance or a new car or new windows for your home. What are the consequences of making the wrong purchasing decision?

What if you are choosing a realtor to sell your home? How high is the risk? It's very high, isn't it? If you choose the wrong company or the wrong person, you could lose a lot of money, couldn't you?

You see, the vast majority of what I refer to as *dysfunctional buying behavior* is a result of perceived high risk. Recall that the higher the risk, the more difficult the purchasing decision becomes; the higher the dollar amount at risk, the more exaggerated the dysfunctional behaviors become.

> WHAT IF YOU COULD MINIMIZE THE RISK TO THE POINT THAT YOUR CUSTOMERS COULD BUY FROM YOU JUST AS EASILY AND EFFORTLESSLY AS YOU BUY A FLASHLIGHT AT WALMART?

What if you could minimize the risk for your prospects? What if you could minimize the risk to the point that your prospect tells you that she doesn't want multiple bids, doesn't want the cheapest price, and doesn't want to think about it for days and weeks on end?

What if you could minimize the risk to the point that your customers could buy from you just as easily and effortlessly as you buy a flashlight at Walmart? Imagine what your sales numbers would look like if your prospect perceived zero risk in buying from you.

There are three simple ways to minimize perceived risk for your prospects and make it easier for them to say yes. You will learn to use each one within the Consistency Selling process.

**THREE SIMPLE WAYS TO
MINIMIZE PERCEIVED RISK**

1. Use your company's guarantees and/or warranties.
2. Use signature stories as the foundation of your sales process.
3. Build a high level of trust.

1. GUARANTEES AND/OR WARRANTIES

Leveraging your company's warranties and guarantees is a very effective way to minimize risk. Many companies offer some type of *risk-reversal* guarantee that is specifically designed to minimize or completely eliminate any perceived risk.

If your product or service does not lend itself to a risk-reversal guarantee, you can use whatever standard guarantees your industry and company has in place. The risk-reversal guarantee is a powerful way to minimize and eliminate risk, but it's not the only way. Even without a risk-reversal guarantee, your company's standard guarantees can be enhanced with a signature story, which we will discuss in the next section.

One of the first examples of a risk-reversal guarantee goes back over 150 years. In 1864, Johannes Badrutt, the founder of the Kulm Hotel in St. Moritz, was faced with the task of attracting visitors to the Swiss Alps long before the area became famous for winter sports. To overcome skepticism about the cold, damp winters, Badrutt offered free lodging if guests did not enjoy their stay. *Furthermore, he would reimburse the guest for travel expenses.* Because there was no risk, Europeans flocked to the Swiss Alps, and the rest, as they say, is history.

Risk-reversal guarantees and risk-minimizing guarantees are powerful ways to minimize risk and drive sales through the roof.

I know many businesses will shy away from such guarantees out of fear, but there is actually very little to be afraid of. Think about it: Suppose you had a customer who was very unhappy about the quality of your product and your service, and you had made every effort to correct the situation. But despite your best efforts, the situation remained unacceptable *even in your opinion.* In other words, you agreed with the customer that the quality was unacceptable.

Eventually the customer demanded her money back or threatened to file a lawsuit, report you to the state's Attorney General's office, call the local news station's consumer affairs reporter, and file a complaint with the BBB. If you knew you had done everything in your power to fix the problem but simply could not fix it *to your standards or the customer's standards,* what would you do?

Dollars to doughnuts, you would refund the customer her money and move on to new opportunities.

And guess what? That's about the only time you would actually have to refund a customer's money, because in most every other case, they will offer you the opportunity to fix the problem, and in most every case, you will be able to do so. And if you couldn't, you'd probably give the customer their money back anyway!

In my heating and air-conditioning company, we had a simple caveat in our guarantee:

"Trust our company with your heating and air-conditioning project, and if you are unhappy for any reason with our service or quality during the first year of ownership, *and we can't fix it to industry standards*, we will cheerfully refund 100 percent of your original investment."

You can always fix it to industry standards! And if you can't, you would refund their money anyway! So if you would do it on the back end in a worst-case scenario, why not promote it on the front end in your sales presentation to minimize risk and close a ton more business at higher margins?

• • •

I remember discussing the risk-reversal strategy with a business owner who scoffed at the idea of offering that kind of guarantee in the heating and air-conditioning industry. "What are you going to do," he asked, "when a homeowner has air-conditioning installed in March and then wants to return it in November?"

I asked, "How many people do you think would actually do something like that?"

He responded, "I don't care if it's one out of a hundred. No one is going to take advantage of me!"

Frustrated, I asked him, "When was the last time a contractor was taken advantage of by a homeowner?"

Blank stare.

So I asked him another simple question: "Does it make more sense to build your company around the 99 percent of honest, hard-working people who just want to be treated fairly or the one crook out of a hundred who would take advantage of the offer?"

Blank stare again.

As it turned out, I opened my own residential heating and air-conditioning company in the same town just a few months later. I was convinced that a risk-reversal guarantee would minimize (if not eliminate) risk and assist me in building a profitable company. I had almost no practical experience in the industry, but I was certain I could succeed if I could use the guarantee (combined with the Prosperity Mindset and my sales process) to earn my customers' business.

The risk-reversal strategy was the foundation of my business plan. As I researched the history of a risk-reversal guarantee and evaluated the potential benefits, I realized how powerful the strategy could be when it is fully committed to and backed by a company. In my estimation, if you could return a drill to Costco, why should it be any different in the heating and air-conditioning business?

> THIS SIMPLE PROMISE TO OUR CUSTOMERS TRANSFORMED MY BUSINESS.

We made the risk-reversal strategy the central component of our sales and marketing strategy in the form of an unconditional "One-Year Test-Drive" on any product or service we sold. We adopted a selling proposition of "100% Right or 100% FREE." This simple promise to our customers transformed my business.

Let me repeat the motto we communicated to our prospects: "Trust our company with your heating and air-conditioning project, and if you are unhappy for any reason with our service or quality during the first year of ownership, and we can't fix it to industry standards, we will cheerfully refund 100% of your original investment."

No tricks. No hassle. Just a simple guarantee to eliminate the risk of making the wrong purchasing decision.

My business exploded. In just sixty months, we generated a total of $20,000,000 in sales and became the largest company of our type in southern Colorado. Over a four-year period we did *twice* as many installations as our nearest competitor, who just happened to be the same guy who scoffed at my idea because he was afraid of the one customer in a hundred who might take advantage of him.

In 2009, my company was selected by *Inc.* magazine as one of the fastest-growing privately held companies in America, and in 2010 I sold the company when I became overwhelmed with offers to train others on what I had learned about growing sales revenue and margins.

Keep in mind, the decision to offer a risk-reversal guarantee is a strategic decision and can only be made by the leadership of your company, because this kind of guarantee requires that your operations and support staff are prepared. The better your operations, the less often you'll have to pay up on the guarantee.

This doesn't mean your operations have to be perfect. It only means that everyone has to understand the obligation of the guarantee. Mistakes will be made; the ball will inevitably be dropped. The key is making sure everyone understands the guarantee when communicating to a customer.

Minimizing risk is not just a warm and fuzzy idea. It is a market-dominating strategy, and the risk-reversal guarantee is just one example of how we can consistently grow our sales volume and margins. If you follow the process I teach in *Consistency Selling*, you will have a systematic and routine way to minimize risk on every lead, every time—whether or not your company offers a risk-reversal guarantee.

Here's one last thing to consider about a risk-reversal strategy: *You cannot evaluate it in the context of your existing sales volume and margins.* The whole point of using a risk-reversal strategy is to dramatically increase conversion rates and margins.

Consider this: Suppose you were buying a new car, and two dealerships had the exact same car. In other words, the car was basically a commodity, as the only difference in the cars was the price.

The car at Dealership A had all the standard manufacturer's warranties. If the transmission or engine or anything else failed, it would be repaired under the warranty at no expense to you.

The car at Dealership B was identical in every way except for one: It included a risk-reversal guarantee. In other words, if the transmission or engine or anything else failed, it would be repaired under the warranty at no expense to you. But in addition to the standard manufacturer warranty, Dealership B allowed you to drive the new car for a year, and if for any reason it did not perform to industry standards during the first year and they could not fix it to perform to industry standards, they would cheerfully refund 100 percent of your original investment.

Which dealership would you buy the car from? Ask yourself this question: How much would you be willing to pay for that peace of mind? Two hundred dollars more? Maybe $500 more?

Regardless of the dollar amount, the reality is you would

most likely buy from Dealership B and pay a slightly higher price for the car in order to buy peace of mind.

The risk-reversal guarantee must be evaluated in the context of increasing your sales volume and margins. And as that happens, *you simply take a small part of each increased sale and put it into a warranty reserve account.* Before you know it, you have tens of thousands of dollars in reserve if you have to refund an unhappy customer.

Even refunding money works to your benefit, because refunding a customer will be the most powerful and effective marketing dollars you'll ever spend. Which brings me to the second way to minimize risk—using Signature Stories.

2. SIGNATURE STORIES

Signature Stories should be used to bring your guarantees to life. Whether your company has a risk-reversal guarantee in place or just the more standard *satisfaction guarantee,* the Signature Story is a vital component to separate your company from the competition and their guarantees.

Keep in mind that your prospects hear about guarantees all the time. They hear about satisfaction guarantees, money-back guarantees, this guarantee, and that guarantee—all day long. There's so much chatter about guarantees that, for most consumers, the noise goes in one ear and out the other. How can you get your message heard? You have to bring the guarantees to life.

A Signature Story is a very effective way to show how

your company and your guarantees actually minimize the risk for customers—and make it easier for them to say yes to you. Signature Stories define the character of your company and provide a way to "prove" how your company responds when the chips are down.

> I ALWAYS LOOK AT UNHAPPY CUSTOMERS
> AS A MARKETING OPPORTUNITY.

During our first few years in business, we had the "opportunity" to "buy back" a few systems that customers were not satisfied with. I say *opportunity* because I always see these situations as marketing opportunities. In most of these cases, we had dropped the ball in serving our customers. Essentially, we had it coming. Even in those situations, we usually issued a partial refund to satisfy the customer. But the letters we got showing how we had met our guarantee were powerful tools in selling the next millions of dollars of products and services. I always look at unhappy customers as a marketing opportunity.

In other situations, however, we had done nothing wrong. Our customer simply needed their money back. And while we were not obligated to refund their money under those circumstances, I viewed each of them as opportunities to prove that my company was willing to do what my competition would never do.

I remember a woman who called me about eight months

after we installed her heating system. She informed me that she had been diagnosed with cancer and was forced to leave her job. As a result, she was forced to sell her home. What she wanted from me was to remove her very expensive high-efficiency system, reinstall a less-expensive system, and refund her the difference.

DOING THE RIGHT THING
ALWAYS PAYS OFF.

Once I understood her situation, I informed her that we would leave her high-efficiency system in place but go ahead and refund her the difference. Not only was it the right thing to do, it was the right business decision, as I would have had new equipment and labor expenses if I replaced her system.

A few months later, she sold her house and wrote us a heart-warming letter outlining what we had done, and how having the high-efficiency system had actually helped her sell the home.

How many millions of dollars' worth of systems do you suppose we sold by sharing that letter with future prospects? I can tell you. It was exactly $20,000,000, because that Signature Story became the foundation of our entire sales process.

Imagine the impact on risk when a customer learns what amazing things we did for customers in a bind. I can't count the times prospects told me things like, "Wow. If you would do that for her, I guess you'll make sure my system is installed properly."

Risk minimized. Sale closed.

That single letter did more to communicate the low risk of dealing with our company than any amount of paid advertising. When our prospects understood there was no risk of making the wrong purchasing decision with our company, it became very easy for them to say yes.

So I strongly urge you to consider the amazing things your company has done for customers and get those stories in writing. All too often I see companies do great things for customers, but they fail to ask for the proof that comes from a letter. Other times, companies get the letters but keep them in a file cabinet collecting dust.

It's crucial for you to get the letters out into the field and integrate them systematically into your sales process. I'll teach you exactly how to use them. If you did something amazing for a customer and failed to get a letter, call them up and ask for one. I don't care if it was two years ago. Call them up and say, "Hey, Mr. Jones, remember when we did that amazing thing for you when our widget didn't perform perfectly? Could you write us a brief letter outlining how we treated you?"

In some cases, your customers want to write a letter but don't because they are too busy or simply don't know what to say. In either case, offer to write the letter for them and take it to them to read and sign.

Just get the damn letter!

Again, I'll teach you exactly how to use the letters in the sales process, but you have to get them first!

A final note on Signature Stories: Your stories *must be in writing*. Any handwritten or typed letter with an original signature is a million times better than a review online. I am not saying online reviews are unimportant, because they're not. Bad reviews can get you ruled out of an opportunity before you even knew there was one. But there is something powerful about an original signature or hand-written letter on paper. Call me old school, but also call me a stone-cold old-school closer, because that's how I roll.

3. TRUST

It is axiomatic that people buy from people they trust. Building trust is the third vital component to minimizing risk and making it easier for your prospects to say yes.

In his groundbreaking book *The Speed of Trust*, Stephen M. R. Covey makes a compelling case that building trust requires two things: character and competence.

We typically think of a trustworthy person as someone who has a good character, but being an honest person is not enough to succeed in sales. You must also have the skills to deliver results and do the job right. Moreover, you have to demonstrate both components to your prospect. They must know you have high character and high competence.

As Covey details in his book, his wife trusts his

character, but when she needed surgery, she chose a surgeon who was competent. You can't let your spouse perform surgery on you just because they are honest. My wife, Taryn, makes a similar argument anytime I want to fix something around the house. She trusts me, but she loves her house—so she calls a professional when she wants something repaired.

• • •

As we go through the Consistency Selling process, we will conduct very specific activities to demonstrate both high character and high competence. Trust isn't built in one single transformational moment; it is built through a consistent demonstration of high character and high competence.

Even if your company doesn't offer risk-reversal guarantees, sales professionals can expertly minimize the risk for prospects by demonstrating high character and high competence and earning the prospects' trust. The Consistency Selling method will show you a systematic way to do this.

> IF YOU WANT TO BE TRULY EFFECTIVE IN SALES, YOU MUST APPROACH SALES FROM A SYSTEMATIC AND STRATEGIC PERSPECTIVE.

These are not random ideas and tactics to be scattered throughout your sales presentation. They must be used in a simple, systematic, and process-driven way. Remember: *Consistent sales activities produce consistent sales results. Random sales activities produce random sales results.*

As I have said many times, you can't focus on consistently doing the right things and accidentally produce the wrong results—and if you want to be truly effective in sales, you must approach sales from a systematic and strategic perspective.

PEOPLE BUY FROM PEOPLE THEY TRUST

We all know that people buy from people they trust. When was the last time you bought something from a salesperson who gave you the creeps? When was the last time a wife said to her husband, "Hey, babe, I met this really creepy guy who made my skin crawl, and I was thinking we should go ahead and buy our windows (or [insert your product here]: siding, life insurance, health insurance, new car, mortgage, air conditioner, furnace, carpet, remodeling, roofing, vacuum cleaner, or textbooks) from him? Or maybe we should let him have our real estate (or [insert your service here]: banking, shipping, accounting, plumbing, or electrical) business!"

If you're like most of us, you'll find every reason to remove yourself from the buying process if the salesperson makes you feel uneasy. Human beings are uncanny in their ability to smell a rat, and when we do, we typically run in the opposite direction. The last thing we do is write them a check or hand them our credit card. Just think about the sales opportunities where we never connected with the prospect or earned their trust. Those calls have predictable endings.

Like I said: People buy from people they trust.

"OK, well that sounds great," your prospect says vaguely at the end of the sales presentation. "Let me give this some thought and figure out our options. I'll give you a call in the next week or so, and we'll get a better idea of how we want to proceed."

Translation: "I don't trust you. I don't trust your work. I don't trust your product and/or service. I don't trust your price."

Knowing that the sinking feeling in your stomach does not bode well for you, you try to pull something more definitive from this sales opportunity. So you say to her, "How about I give you a call back next Tuesday morning and follow up to see if you have any other questions?"

"Sure," the prospect responds.

Translation: "Sure, give me a call and send a few emails. I won't respond to either."

And the only thing emptier than her words is the feeling you get when you see your commission check. You know she won't be calling you next week. You know she won't be returning your calls. You know this deal is dead.

Of course, we've all had the polar-opposite experience, too. You know the situation I'm talking about, don't you? The situation where the conversation and communication with your prospect is effortless and sincere and when trust comes naturally—and when your prospect signs on the dotted line, you are not the least bit surprised.

In that situation, the outcome is equally clear. You know it's going to be a done deal; when you reach the end of your sales presentation, you make recommendations that your prospect readily accepts, you write up the paperwork, and the transaction ends as smoothly as it began.

Translation: "I trust you. I trust your work. I trust your product and/or service. I trust your price."

Most of us have had both of these experiences.

But here's the rub: Many of us operate on the misguided assumption that the quality of the relationship and trust with a prospect is more or less predetermined before we even start the sales call. In other words, we believe some prospects are going to trust us, and others are not.

SOME DAYS, WE ARE THE DOG

"That's just the way it is," we tell ourselves. Some days we are the dog, and some days we are the fire hydrant. We essentially go from sales call to sales call discovering which prospects are going to trust us and which prospects are not.

Here is a news flash, my friend: That kind of thinking is going to keep you in perpetual sales purgatory and financial hell.

You see, you are not at the mercy of random good or bad relationships on a sales call. You are not a victim of happenstance. Trust is not an arbitrary thing that you either have or you don't have. Every situation has unique potential to improve communication and earn the trust and business of your prospect.

You have the ability to influence whether or not a prospect grows to trust you or not. Of course, you don't control the prospect's ultimate decision about buying from you, but there are specific things you can do to earn your prospect's trust. Even if things get off to a slow and uncomfortable start, you have the ability to change the prospect's mind by demonstrating high character and high competence and earning trust.

You are not a powerless person who is dependent on circumstances and the luck of the draw to determine your financial prosperity and security. Trust is not random. You can earn it. And the more skilled you become at earning it, the more income you will earn. Period.

But trust doesn't happen in an instant. Just as in your personal relationships, trust accumulates over time as people evaluate your sincerity and trustworthiness. You didn't earn 100 percent of your spouse's trust on the first date. He or she made an initial evaluation based on countless variables and then decided whether or not there was a basis to move further down the line. Eventually, your spouse decided you were trustworthy, and the relationship blossomed. In the absence of that trust, you would still be single.

Trust accumulates (or not) over the course of a sales

call. It happens (or not) over a much shorter amount of time, but the same rules that govern personal relationships govern sales relationships.

TRUST IS BUILT LITTLE BY LITTLE

Trust is built little by little, one brick at a time. Think about building trust on a sales call the way an attorney thinks about circumstantial evidence in a legal proceeding. In a circumstantial case, there is no single piece of evidence that proves the case. Unlike a physical evidence case, there are no fingerprints, DNA, or videos to definitively determine what happened. There is no Perry Mason moment.

In a circumstantial case, the arguments are made one brick at a time. No single brick is determinative, but the accumulation of many bricks (coincidences) eventually builds a "wall of evidence" that allows reasonable people to draw conclusions. For example, suppose a prosecutor has accused a defendant in a murder case, and you are on the jury. The prosecutor shows that a car matching the defendant's car was seen in the neighborhood of the murder victim.

So what? you think to yourself. *There were probably lots of cars that match the defendant's car in that part of town.* Yes, that is true, but a bystander got a look at the first three letters of the murderer's license plate, and those three letters match the defendant's license plate.

Big deal, you say to yourself. *There are lots of similar cars with a few matching letters on the license plate.* That is also true, but cell phone records show that the defendant's phone pinged off a cell tower just blocks away from the murder scene at about the time of the murder.

Whatever. It's not a crime to be in that neighborhood, you think, as your suspicion grows. Yes, but another witness has come forward and stated that the defendant threatened to kill the victim a week before the murder.

Oh. That dude is guilty as sin.

You see, at some point there are just too many coincidences, and brick by brick, the prosecutor has built the wall of evidence that leads to only one logical conclusion: The defendant is guilty.

Similarly, prospects reach logical conclusions over the time of the sales process, and while there may be no single piece of evidence that determines their conclusions, brick by brick a case is made about whether or not they will trust you.

And whether or not that wall of evidence supports or undermines your prospect's conclusion to trust you is well within your ability to influence. The wall of trust (or distrust) is not random. You are not at the mercy of uncontrollable events.

You just need a reliable process designed to build trust. And that is exactly what a systematic sales process will give you. It is a process designed to eliminate doubt about you and your products and services. It is based on trust, built one brick at a time, until eventually you have built a wall of evidence that leads your prospect to only one logical conclusion: They can trust you.

WILL YOU TRUST ME?

When we are finished with the sales presentation, you will be prepared to ask one simple question: "Will you trust me?" Everything you ever needed to know about sales and creating financial prosperity is contained within those four simple words. Yet many sales professionals seek to convince, cajole, and connive prospects into becoming customers in a way that resembles conflict rather than harmony. There is a better, less stressful way to create transformational results in your sales profession.

Once you have earned the right to ask that simple question without feeling awkward or unnatural, you will know you have done your job. If you get to the end of your sales process and you do not feel comfortable asking that question, you have not sufficiently earned the right to ask the question—and you have failed at your job. If asking the question doesn't feel natural and comfortable, you can rest assured you have not even come close to earning your prospect's trust.

After all, you can't walk into a sales call, hastily offer solutions to problems you have not thoroughly diagnosed, offer your prospect a cheap price, and comfortably ask, "Will you trust me with these recommendations?"

It wouldn't make sense. It wouldn't feel natural. You

would look and sound like a pushy moron. On the other hand, if you go on a sales call and gradually and systematically build a relationship with your prospect, take the time to identify their problems and the appropriate solutions, and demonstrate your integrity and competence, you will have earned the right to ask that simple question: "Will you trust me with these recommendations?"

If it feels right, it is. If it doesn't, it isn't. Everything you do on a sales call must move you one step closer to being able to naturally and comfortably ask that question. In the immortal words of the late Dr. Stephen R. Covey, "If you are trustworthy, you will be trusted."

But to minimize risk, even trustworthy people need a systematic way to demonstrate they are trustworthy. Even trustworthy people need to approach the sales process from a strategic perspective and keep an eye toward being able to ask a simple question at the end of the sales presentation: "Will you trust me?"

In summary, it's critically important to minimize risk for your prospects during every sales opportunity. The combination of systematically using your company's warranties and guarantees, leveraging a signature story, and demonstrating high character and high competence to earn trust will play a significant role in improving your sales results and growing your income. That's the good news. The great news is that the information in the next chapter is going to completely transform your sales career and permanently change your zip code.

CHAPTER 5

THE SALES HALLWAY

I use the term *sales hallway* as a metaphor for what happens on a sales call. From the moment you initiate contact with a prospect to the moment you either lose or win their business, you are in the sales hallway. The sales hallway is a good way to understand some of the frustrating things that can happen on a sales call.

Imagine yourself standing at the beginning of a long hallway with your prospect. At the far end of the hallway is a door. If you can get your prospect to the door, you win the deal. That is, if you successfully navigate the sales hallway, solve your prospect's problems, and earn their trust, you can escort them through the distant door where you earn their business.

Of course, it's not quite that easy, because in addition

to the door at the far end of the hallway that represents getting the sale, the hallway is lined with other doors along either side. Those doors represent escape routes for your prospects, which allow them to derail the sales process by exiting the sales hallway,

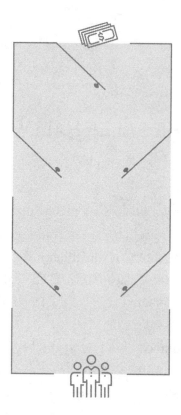

In many cases, your prospects don't want to be engaged in the sales process at all. Perhaps they have had a bad experience with a salesperson in the past, or maybe they simply believe the sales process usually ends with them

being separated from their hard-earned money. But in any case, there are a thousand places they would rather be than in the sales hallway with you.

So here is what often happens: As you walk with your prospect down the sales hallway, he is gathering as much information as he can about you, your company, your products and services—and most of all, information about your *price*. And once your prospect gets all the information he wants, he makes every effort to exit the hallway through one of the side doors so he can do can do the most human thing imaginable: Postpone the pain of spending money.

Spending money causes emotional pain for most of us, so we postpone making a buying decision as long as possible. Think about it. If you have the choice between spending money today and spending it next week, when would you rather spend it? It's just human nature—we like to keep our money in our pockets as long as we can.

Once your prospect has all the information he wants (especially the price), there are very specific words that come out of his mouth to allow him to get out of the sales hallway. You hear them every day of your professional life, and if you are not prepared to deal with them, your prospects will effectively use them to end the sales process. When that happens, the sales call concludes with uncertainty, and you end up waiting for a call next Tuesday, which never comes.

Typically, the words your prospect uses to derail and/ or terminate the sales process sound something like this:

I want more bids/proposals.

I want a cheaper price.

I want/need to think/sleep/talk/pray about it.

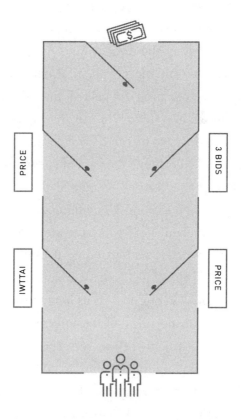

So there you are, walking with your prospect down the sales hallway, and everything seems like it's going great when all of a sudden your prospect says, "Well, now, that all sounds really great, but my wife and I will need some time to think about it. We never make quick decisions."

BAM! He is out of the hallway, and the next thing

you know, you are handing him a business card, and he's promising he'll call you next Tuesday. And unless you still believe in Santa Claus and the Easter Bunny, you know that next Tuesday never comes. Soon, your prospect is ignoring your emails and your phone calls.

Or maybe you are sailing down the sales hallway with the sun in your face and the wind at your back, and you just know this deal is in the bag. Then suddenly, your prospect says, "Well, that all seems to make sense, but I've got another company I am talking to tomorrow. Let me talk to them, and I'll get back with you and let you know what we decide."

BAM! Out of the hallway again! Next thing you know, you are scrambling to find out who the other company is, and you start trying to wheel and deal, even though you know you are sounding a little desperate and borderline pathetic.

Maybe your prospect loves you and your company, and just when you think it's a done deal, she says, "You guys sound great, but I just can't afford your price. I am going to have to choose the other company, because they are quite a bit cheaper. Unless, of course, you can do a little better on your price."

So you start reminding the prospect of your value and the difference between price and cost—and any other technique you've learned over the years—but deep down, you know it's over. You know in your heart it's another lost opportunity.

THERE HAS TO BE A BETTER WAY

Alas, the sales professional is left standing alone in the hallway with shattered dreams of that big commission. As the prospect slips out one of the doors, she assures the sales professional all is not lost, and she will call back on Tuesday. The sales professional sheepishly holds out hope against all hope, tells his manager he "feels good about this one," and clings to the fairy tale that the prospect will actually call him back.

As a sales professional, you are probably saying to yourself, *There has to be a better way.*

Fortunately, there is.

Traditional sales training teaches us to proceed through the sales process (hallway), and when we get to the end, we ask for the order. If the prospect has an objection, we respond with a rebuttal. If she has another objection, we fire back with another rebuttal. Objection. Rebuttal. Objection. Rebuttal. Before you know it, things start resembling a tennis match with all the back-and-forth. Furthermore, this kind of scenario can start to feel stressful, combative, and almost adversarial.

Keep in mind that tension is necessary on a sales call. If there is no tension, you are most likely not asking the tough questions to close the opportunity. *But there should never be conflict on a sales call.* The prospect wins the conflict situation every time. Sometimes the back-and-forth of objection/rebuttal can feel like conflict, which is never in your best interest.

Consider this: When are tensions the highest on a sales call—at the beginning or at the end when we start talking about the money? At the end, right? As soon as we start talking about money, things seem to tighten up and tensions start to mount.

Well, I'm no rocket scientist, but if the tension is highest at the end of the sales presentation, that seems like a really bad time to use rebuttals to convince prospects that they don't "need to think about it," they shouldn't "get another bid," or they don't "need a cheaper price." At that point, it's already too late. By the time you've overcome their second objection, they've gone to DEFCON 1, and you'll have a hard time getting them to agree that the sky is blue.

There has to be a better way, you say to yourself again.

There is.

With a little foresight, planning, and key questions, the sales professional can seal the hallway doors closed as he escorts the prospect past them. When the doors are sealed properly, the prospect will be faced with no escape routes and will be left with his only other option—answering yes or no when the sales professional asks for the order. And as I will demonstrate later, *yes is best, but no is a perfectly acceptable answer.*

"No" will not hurt you in sales. "I don't know" will destroy you.

The key is to securely close the doors as you navigate the sales hallway. By doing this, the prospect will make certain public declarations and help you close the doors and eliminate their own escape routes. When the escape routes are closed, the prospect is infinitely more likely to make a yes or no decision with you talking directly to them. And when your prospect does make a yes or no decision with you sitting in front of them, the decision will most often be yes, because prospects don't like to reject you face-to-face or directly over the phone.

Keep in mind that you will always get one of two answers at the end of the sales process—either a yes or a no. If the answer is yes, your prospect is signing something. *Everything else is a no.*

WHEN A YES IS A NO

In many cases, a prospect can make a no sound like a yes, but no is still no unless they sign something. A no disguised as a yes might sound like this: "I really like your company, and I think we are going to go with you. Why don't you swing by next week, and we'll do the paperwork?"

That is a no cleverly disguised as a yes.

With few exceptions, most human beings simply do not like conflict; therefore, they do not want to say no to your face or on the phone. They want to say no by not returning your calls and emails. But if you leverage consistency, build trust, and close the hallway doors, prospects will be more likely to make a final decision about you and your company with you in front of them. And as I've mentioned previously, when prospects make a final decision with you in front of them, that final decision will likely be a yes.

Obviously, this doesn't mean that every call will be a one-call close. It simply means that there comes a point in every sales opportunity where it's time for the rubber to meet the road. Whether it's a one-call close or a two-year sales cycle, there comes a time when your prospect has to make a final decision. If at all possible, you want to be sitting in front of them when they make it.

But how do you systematically close the doors in the hallway?

That is a great question, and it's at the heart of Consistency Selling.

• • •

Up to this point in our discussion, I have referred to *consistency* as the concept of a sales professional repeating the same process on every sales opportunity in an effort to produce consistent sales results.

But to truly understand the power of this process, it's necessary to understand the Consistency Principle as developed by Dr. Robert Cialdini.

The Consistency Principle stands for the proposition that "public declarations dictate future actions." In essence, human beings have a tendency to act in a manner consistent with their words.

I remember the light bulb moment I had while reading an article in *Scientific American* written by Dr. Cialdini.

Within the article were a few paragraphs that completely changed my financial fortunes. I am not overstating it by saying that I attribute a huge amount of the financial success I have achieved to what I learned in these few paragraphs.

The article discussed a common problem for restaurants: People make reservations and then fail to cancel the reservations even though they aren't going to actually show up.

Obviously, this causes problems of cash flow and capacity for a restaurant. Imagine the restaurant has a reservation for an eight-top table for 7:00 p.m. At 6:45 p.m., another party of eight shows up without a reservation and wants the table. The host cannot accommodate them because of the reservation. The party of eight leaves the restaurant and takes their business to a competitor down the street. The 7:00 p.m. reservation is a no-call, no-show—they fail to cancel their reservation—and the result is lost revenue and cash flow for the restaurant.

In an effort to avoid this, the restaurant's process had been to remind customers to "please call if you have to change your plans." Yet despite having reservations agents remind customers to call if they could not make their reservation, the restaurant still experienced a 30 percent "no-call/no-show" rate.

However, the restaurant cited in this article made one small change that had an enormous impact. They simply added two words to their process. Instead of saying, "Please call if you have to change your plans," they added two words and framed their request as a question, rather than a request: *"Will you* please call if you have to change your plans?"

The reservations agent then paused until the customer said, "Yes."

The no-call/no-show rate immediately went from 30 percent to 10 percent! That's an improvement of 66.66 percent! *That means that two out of three people felt obligated to take actions consistent with their public declarations.* That represents a massively significant percentage of people who were motivated by the Consistency Principle.

LEVERAGE HUMAN NATURE

Another example in the article outlined how a company that did fundraising *doubled monetary contributions* by having potential donors sign a petition supporting the cause prior to being asked for a contribution.

These numbers were staggering in my mind. I instantly realized I could earn a fortune in sales and business by leveraging human nature. I began to wonder what would happen if I could get my prospects to publicly declare the following:

· "I prefer your company over getting three
  bids/proposals."

· "There are more important factors than getting
  the cheapest price."

· "I can let you know today whether or not your company is a good fit."

I immediately began designing questions and scenarios within my sales process to influence my prospects to make those public declarations. The results were as staggering as those described in the article. Not only did I notice that the amount of "closing conflict" was dramatically reduced, but my sales results exploded. I quickly learned how accurate Dr. Cialdini really was. My customers began to routinely take action consistent with their declarations to me.

I also began to wonder if the Consistency Principle could work *against me* if I didn't leverage it properly. I thought about the conversations my customers were having just before I arrived on the sales opportunity. I realized that in many cases my prospects were telling each other, "Honey, we are not buying tonight! We are not going to make a quick decision. We are getting three bids and a cheap price!"

If customers are having those conversations (or similar ones), what actions are they going to take that are consistent with *those* public declarations at the end of the sales process? Exactly! Even if you've done a great job, they will take actions consistent with those declarations and postpone the decision, get three bids/proposals, and make the decision based on price.

You cannot allow a prospect's internal discussions about postponing the purchasing decision, getting three bids/

proposals, and price to be the last things they say! If you are going to be successful in sales, you must strategically find a way to influence your prospects and get them to make different public declarations that are consistent with having them buy from you.

During the process, you will proactively take a look behind each hallway door and have honest discussions about what's behind it ("I want to think about it," "I want a cheaper price," and "I want multiple bids/proposals"). Once you've had an open and honest conversation about each concern, you simply ask the appropriate questions to close the door and move on down the hallway.

You will notice that objections are the same as the ones you typically face at the end of the sales process. My contention is simply that you should handle them *before the prospect brings them up* as you walk casually down the hallway. Because you already know the objections are behind the doors, you can address them proactively. And with a few simple exercises, questions, and "third-party verifiers," you can seal the doors shut.

If the prospect tries to reopen the door at the end in an effort to escape from the hallway, you can politely and respectfully remind him that the issue has already been addressed. You can further remind the prospect that he closed the door himself,

I can hear many of you protesting, "I've always been taught to *never* bring up an objection unless and until the prospect brings it up first!" Simply stated, I completely disagree with that sales philosophy. And I have successfully taught and watched this process produce powerful sales results in hundreds of other companies, including FedEx, Farmers Insurance, The Home Depot, Mitsubishi Electric, Carrier Corp., and many others. As far as I'm concerned, the proof is in the sales pudding.

Here is the thing: If your prospects don't bring up price, do you really believe they haven't thought about it? Do you really believe they aren't considering a less expensive option? If the prospect doesn't bring up competitive offers, do you really believe he is not thinking about evaluating your competitors?

The bottom line is that your prospects are more informed and sophisticated than ever, thanks to the Internet. Whether or not they bring up price or competitive offers or any other issue, they are thinking about them. *Ignore that at your own peril!*

DON'T PLAY SALES TENNIS

If you wait to deal with them when they bring their objections up at the end, it will be too late. They know you are trying to close them at that point, and you will come off sounding defensive. That's old-school sales—they raise an objection, and you combat it with a rebuttal. They raise another objection, and you combat it with another rebuttal. Remember: It's like sales tennis. Back and forth. Back and forth.

Addressing the inevitable objections early on and getting the prospect's agreement about the issue will prove far more persuasive. If you address price only after the prospect raises the issue, they will see what you're doing. If, however, you address price early in the conversation, the prospect will be far more inclined to agree with you about the dangers of a cheap price. Try to get them to agree that price is not the most important issue when you are asking them to sign an agreement.

IF THE FIRST TIME PRICE COMES UP IS AT THE END OF THE PROCESS, IT'S TOO LATE.

Once you get your prospect to agree with you about price, they will be far more likely to act in a manner consistent with that public declaration. If the first time price comes up is at the end of the process, it's too late. If competitive bids come up for the first time at the end of the process, it's too late. If the prospect's attempt to postpone the purchasing decision comes up for the first time at the end, it is too late.

Any issues that will potentially come up at the end of the hallway have to be uncovered, discussed, and resolved *as you walk down the hallway—not at the end when your prospect may have adopted a defensive posture.*

The objective here is to prepare yourself for the inevitable issues regarding price, competitors, or anything else that will come up at the end of the hallway. If an issue has been left unresolved, that door has effectively been left open, and your prospect may decide to exit the hallway through it. If all the issues behind the doors have been addressed (and the doors closed), you can hold your prospect accountable to what they previously agreed to. The results, as you will see, are astounding.

MONSTERS IN THE CLOSET

Here is another way to look at the process. Imagine your young son or daughter starts screaming, "There's a monster in the closet!" in the middle of the night. When you enter your child's bedroom, do you begin yelling, "Get out! Run for your life before it eats you!"? Hopefully not, although the prospect of having some fun with your kid will be tempting to the practical jokers out there.

Aside from the practical jokers, what most of us would do is walk over to the closet, open the door all the way, and turn on the closet light. Once you show your child that the "monster" is just a pile of laundry, and you are convinced that she is convinced there is nothing to be afraid of, you turn out the light and securely close the closet door. Once she is assured there's nothing there, you tuck her back in and go down the hall to your bedroom.

It's the same way with our prospects. Often they see an issue they perceive as something to be afraid of behind one of the open doors—maybe it's the price monster or maybe it's the competitive bid monster. Our job is to take the prospect by the hand, walk them over to the closet, open the door all the way, and turn the light on. Once you have exposed the truth, and your prospect understands that there is nothing to be afraid of, you turn the light off, close the door, and move on down the hallway to the next door.

Suppose the prospect sees a "price monster" behind the first door. You walk over to the door, open it all the way, and turn the light on. To shed some light on the price monster, you might say, "You know, Mr. Prospect, you are probably thinking you need a cheap price. Is that fair to say?"

Your prospect might reply, "Oh yeah, I am definitely looking for a great price!"

To which you might say, "Now, are you looking for the down and dirtiest, cheapest price with no regard for quality and service, or are you looking for a great value—a fair price with outstanding quality and service?"

Almost always, the prospect will respond, "Oh yes, a great value. That's what I want."

Keep in mind that even if your prospect cares about nothing but a cheap price, he will be inclined to agree with you about value over price.

You could then agree by saying, "I agree, Mr. Prospect. It really is about value, isn't it? In fact, take a look at this article from the ABC Industry Trade magazine. On page 34, it says the most important factor when buying widget A or service B is finding the best provider. Why do you suppose they say that?"

(I will show you later how easy it is to find "third-party verification" from an industry source that will support your contention that there is more to consider than price alone. It is *critical* that you find it and use third-party verification.)

The prospect may respond with something like, "I don't know. I guess each provider is different. Some are better than others."

"Exactly, Mr. Prospect. In fact, suppose a competitor came along with a similar product and a cheaper price but inferior quality. If the product lasted half as long as mine, would they really have saved you any money?"

Mr. Prospect answers, "I guess not."

"So let me ask you this, Mr. Prospect. Do you agree or disagree with ABC Industry Trade magazine that finding the best provider is the most important thing—maybe even more important than price?"

"I guess so," says Mr. Prospect.

Keep in mind, this is very early on in the process, and the prospect is not experiencing as much trepidation as he will at the closing. Right now, you are empathizing about price with him, and there is not even a hint of closing. You're just having a casual conversation about price.

In this scenario, I have effectively gotten Mr. Prospect to make a public declaration and agree with my point that price is not the most important consideration, and I did it with a few questions and using third-party verification. Moreover, I am having the conversation early on in the sales hallway, so my prospect is not stressing about me trying to close him. I have effectively closed that door, and now my prospect is more inclined to take actions consistent with his public declaration, which is to make the purchasing decision on factors other than a cheap price.

As you walk down the hallway, you realize the prospect sees the "multiple-bid monster" behind it. At that door you might say, "Mr. Prospect, you might be considering getting multiple proposals on this purchase. Is that the case?"

Once he agrees, you shine some light on the issue and demonstrate why it's not necessary to get multiple offers (using industry third-party verification, a few simple questions, and letters from other customers). Once you know the prospect is convinced that the importance of getting three bids is a myth, you turn the light out, close the door, and move on down the hall.

By proactively getting your prospect to agree that price is not the most important issue and that multiple bids are unnecessary, you'll find that the prospect is more likely to make a purchasing decision that is consistent with those declarations.

TAKE YOUR TIME

It's crucial to take your time when you are walking down the sales hallway, getting your prospect to make certain public declarations, and preparing yourself for the closing sequence. All the while, you are engaging in activities designed to demonstrate high character and high competence.

If you rush to the end of the hallway and have failed to prepare yourself, you'll be left empty-handed at the close and have only a hope and a prayer of the prospect calling you back. Listen—I am all about positive thinking and hope, but try feeding your family on those two dishes.

BUILD TRUST, AND COMMIT TO A STORY

As I said earlier, a primary objective for us is to leverage trust and consistency as we proceed through the sales process. The following example illustrates why trust and consistency are so powerful. Suppose law enforcement personnel are investigating an assault that occurred on a Saturday night at 7:00 p.m. They have a suspect who was just brought in for questioning, and because the investigators are really smart, they leverage trust and consistency to crack the case.

Once the suspect is in the interrogation room, the cops begin to build trust with him. And although the suspect is skeptical, he can't help himself. He is, after all, only human. So, when the cops offer him a cigarette and a cup of coffee, he accepts them—and by doing so, he has immediately lowered his defenses. These cops seem like really good guys.

As the cops and suspect become "friends," the tensions lessen. The cops even *seem* to understand that deep down the suspect is a good person. They go so far as telling him, "Now, we know you're a good guy, and there is no way you callously assaulted the victim. I mean, he probably said or did something that set you off, right?"

Our suspect can't believe it! These cops are actually sympathetic to him. They listen to and seem to understand him. They know deep down he is still that little boy on the playground who just lost his way. They probably even understand that he doesn't deserve prison for this lapse in judgment that led to his assaulting the victim. Maybe they'll eventually let him go free!

Once the cops practice a few trust behaviors (straight talk, showing respect, listening), they ask the suspect to account for his whereabouts over the weekend. At this point, it doesn't matter if the suspect is truthful or not. The cops simply want him to commit to a story, because when they are done, another cop is going to come in the interrogation room and ask the same questions.

And this process will continue until what happens?

That's right! (You've been watching too many murder mysteries!) The cops will continue the process until the suspect changes his story. And the moment the suspect changes his story (becomes inconsistent), the cops are going to say, "Wait a minute, earlier you said you were across town at 7:00 p.m.!" And at that moment, the cops know they've got him, and the suspect knows the same thing.

• • •

In sales, we don't have *suspects*, but we do have *prospects*.

And what works for cops to solve a crime will work for us to solve the mystery of selling! All we have to do is build trust and get our prospects to commit to a story. If they change their story later on, we simply hold them accountable for their previous statements. And the story we are going to get our prospects to commit to has three parts.

THREE PARTS OF THE STORY
YOUR PROSPECT MUST COMMIT TO

1. Finding a reliable company that is competent and trustworthy is more important than getting multiple bids/proposals.
2. Price is not the most important consideration in the purchasing decision.
3. A definitive decision about you and your company can be made without unnecessary delay.

Once we have gotten our prospect to commit to their story (thereby closing the escape-route doors), *then and only then* do we ask for the order. And because all the doors are closed, the prospect is inclined to take an action consistent with their previous declarations by making a decision. And because you have taken the time to build trust and show that your company is competent and reliable (and you are sitting in front of or are on the phone with the prospect when he makes the final decision), the answer is far more likely to be yes than no.

So the sales hallway is the metaphor we have used for the sales process. As we navigate the hallway, we build the relationship, investigate our prospect's problems, sell our company's solutions to those problems, and then conclude the process by asking the prospect, "Will you trust me with these recommendations?"

As we are engaging the prospects, we are interweaving seven Power Questions throughout the presentation. These questions are designed to influence the prospect to make certain public declarations that are consistent with purchasing from us.

WALKING DOWN THE SALES HALLWAY

In summary, within the R.I.S.C. steps you will use the seven Power Questions to ensure your prospect makes public declarations consistent with buying from you. You will also engage in specific activities designed to earn trust through high character and high competence.

Consistency Selling allows you to take your prospect's hand and walk them down the sales hallway. As you navigate the hallway, you will follow the R.I.S.C. steps, build trust, and ask the Power Questions.

Your prospect's answers to the Power Questions will have them making public declarations consistent with buying from you. When combined with a high level of trust, those answers render your prospect more likely to take actions consistent with those declarations.

THE FOUR STEPS OF CONSISTENCY SELLING—R.I.S.C.

· RELATIONSHIP building
· INVESTIGATE problems
· SELL your company and your solutions
· CONCLUDE the sales opportunity

As you become more skilled at navigating the sales hallway, earning trust, and closing doors, you will see increased sales productivity. At the end of the hallway, the streets are paved with gold. Once you get there on a consistent basis, you will change your zip code and have fat, happy little kids.

PART TWO

In Part Two, it's time to get down to learning the powerful R.I.S.C. process. Within each step, you will learn the following:

1. The core skill of each step and its importance in overall sales success.

2. Key Trust-Building Objectives designed to demonstrate high character and/or high competence.

3. The relevant Power Questions to close the doors as you navigate the sales hallway.

In the "RELATIONSHIP building" step (part one), you will learn the key Trust-Building Objective of using company guarantees and your signature story to demonstrate high character and how to ask Power Question #1 to close the "I need multi-proposals" door.

In the "RELATIONSHIP building" step (part two), you will learn the key Trust-Building Objective of demonstrating high competency by using third-party experts to show your company meets or exceeds the highest industry standards and how to ask Power Question #2 to close the "I need a cheaper price" door.

In the "INVESTIGATE the problem" step you will learn the key Trust-Building Objective of demonstrating high competency by conducting a comprehensive and systematic diagnosis to investigate your prospect's problems and how to ask Power Question #3 to close the "I want to think about it" door.

In the "SELL your company and solutions" step, you will learn the key Trust-Building Objective of demonstrating high competency by presenting a compelling picture of your company and conducting a product/service demonstration to show that your company is trustworthy. You will also learn how to ask Power Questions #4, #5, and #6 to permanently change the price dynamic.

Finally, in the "CONCLUDE the call" step, you will learn the key Trust-Building Objective of demonstrating high competency by making specific recommendations for solutions to solve the prospect's unique problems and how to leverage the prospect's public declarations to bring the call to a conclusion by asking Power Question #7 and CLOSING THE OPPORTUNITY.

CHAPTER 6

RELATIONSHIP BUILDING (PART 1)— BUILD TRUST, AND CLOSE THE "I NEED MULTI-PROPOSALS" DOOR

In this chapter, you will learn how to build trust by using your company's guarantees and a signature customer story to demonstrate how you treat your customers when the chips are down.

Additionally, you will set the first consistency anchor by asking Power Question #1 and having your prospect make the public declaration that they would prefer choosing your company over getting multiple proposals from other companies. This closes the "I need multiple proposals" door.

Key Trust-Building Objective: Use company guarantees and your signature story to demonstrate high character.

Key Consistency Anchor: Ask Power Question #1, and close the multi-proposal door.

Here is a quick outline of the conversation in part one of Relationship Building:

- Engage in traditional relationship-building conversations (asking questions, showing genuine interest, etc.) and share basic information about your company.
- Address any perceived weaknesses of your company or product or service.
- Discuss how your company's guarantees are designed to minimize risk, and then share your signature story (demonstrate high character).
- Ask the prospect about their previous experiences with getting multiple proposals and discuss the "three-bid myth."
- Ask Power Question #1 to close the multi-proposal door (set consistency anchor).

In this chapter, you will begin building the wall of evidence that will prove your company is the best choice for your prospect. This will be accomplished by using your company's guarantees and signature story to demonstrate how your company treats customers, both of which demonstrate high character. You will then leverage your signature story to set a consistency anchor by getting your prospect to declare that they prefer a trustworthy company like yours over getting multiple bids/proposals.

While building a relationship with your prospects is fundamental to the selling process, you are probably already quite good at it. It's typically the first thing we learn to do in sales. Although the phrase "people buy from those they like and trust" is an often-used cliché, it is also very true. Because relationship building is the first step as you enter the sales hallway with your prospect, it is also your first opportunity to lay the foundation for sales success and prepare yourself for the endgame of asking for your prospect's trust.

STEP ONE: ENGAGE IN TRADITIONAL RELATIONSHIP-BUILDING CONVERSATIONS

Building a relationship with your prospect always begins with getting them to like you and identifying commonalities if you can. The best way to accomplish both of these is with questions, questions, and questions. There's no better way to get people to like you than to show genuine interest in them, and there's no better way to show genuine interest in others than by asking questions. While it is axiomatic to talk about things you have in common like fishing, motorcycles, or golf, it is critical to keep the conversation about *their* fishing, *their* motorcycles, or *their* golf—not yours. If you respond to your prospect's golf stories with your own, it may sound like you are trying to one-up them.

KEEP THEM IN THE SPOTLIGHT

When opening the conversation with your prospect, imagine the two of you are seated in a dark room where a spotlight shines on the person doing the talking—but there is only *one* spotlight, and it can't be on both of you at the same time. Your responsibility is to keep the spotlight on the other person. Anytime you feel the heat and the glare of the spotlight on you, you've got to get it back on your prospect. The most effective way to do that is by asking them a question. Keep the spotlight on them with questions about them. Here is an example of what I mean.

In 2004, I was one year out of prison and found myself on a plane to Maui. As I made the daylong trek across the Pacific Ocean, I could hardly believe my good fortune. For seven years, in my prison cell, one of the things on my Prosperity Plan was "I am writing a book on the beaches of Maui." When I landed on Maui, I picked up a rental car, and as I drove to the hotel, I looked to my right and saw the Kapalua Resort butterfly logo. *Holy cow!* I thought. *That's*

Kapalua! That's where the Plantation Course is! That's where the PGA has the Mercedes-Benz Championship!

In 2000, the Plantation Course had played host to one of the most exciting PGA event finishes I had ever seen. Tiger Woods and Ernie Els had battled it out that Sunday afternoon in a thrilling match that went back and forth. Eventually, Tiger won the tournament with a birdie on the second hole of sudden death. I had watched the tournament from my prison cell just four years earlier. I couldn't believe I would soon have the chance to play the same course that once seemed a million miles and a dozen lifetimes away.

A few days later, I stood atop the number-one tee box looking down at the perfectly manicured fairway and across the Pacific toward Molokai. It was even more spectacular than I had imagined—even in my wildest dreams. I looked down at my feet and thought, *Wow, Tiger and Ernie teed off from this same spot!* Then, of course, I realized they had actually teed off from the tee box about a hundred and fifty yards farther back. But it was close enough for me!

As I played golf that day, I imagined I was walking with Tiger and Ernie. I was seeing the same things they had seen and was walking the same course. I couldn't believe how much my life had changed in such a short time. Walking down the number-eighteen fairway, I imagined what it would feel like to walk down to the cheering Sunday galleries. It was a special day and a special round of golf that will stick with me forever.

A few days later, I was back home and going on my

first sales opportunity after vacation. What do you suppose I saw as I entered the prospect's home? That's right: golf stuff everywhere. Immediately I knew where I would find common ground with my prospect. As we began the obligatory chitchat about golf, I bit my tongue until it nearly bled. There was no way I was going to talk about my trip to Maui and the amazing experience I had at the Plantation Course. How do you suppose that would have sounded to my prospect?

Over the course of that sales opportunity, we talked a lot about golf. But we talked about *his* golf. *His* courses. *His* golf vacations. It was all I could do, but I kept the spotlight on my prospect. If you struggle with finding questions to ask your prospect in the early chitchat stage, here is an easy reminder to help you—and one that I am pretty sure I read in a Zig Ziglar book: It's the acronym FORM, which stands for Family, Occupation, Recreation, and Material Possessions. Ask a prospect about any of these, and with a little probing, you'll be surprised how the conversation will take off.

For example:

You: "So, is your family from here (Family)?"

Prospect: "No, we're actually from back East."

You: "Really? How did you end up out here?"

Prospect: "My dad was transferred out here when I was a teenager."

You: "No kidding. What line of work was your dad in (*Occupation*)?"

Prospect: "He worked for the railroad."

You: "How in the world did he end up in that line of business?"

From that point, there is no telling where the conversation will go. Sometimes you'll be lucky enough to have your prospect start talking about something he is really excited about. When that happens, just let him run with it—the longer the better.

DON'T FORCE THE ISSUE

As a cautionary note, keep in mind that if the early rapport-building starts getting awkward, don't force the issue. Relationship building often happens over the course of the sales process. It might not happen right on cue in the beginning. Many prospects are skeptical of the mindless chitchat that takes place in the early stages, and it may require a little more patience and waiting for the right opportunity. If you sense that your prospect isn't interested in small talk, move on to something more appropriate. Just keep in mind that whatever you talk about initially, make it about them. You'll have plenty of time to talk about your company and your solution. Keep the spotlight where it belongs—on your prospect.

Ask questions, take a genuine interest in the prospect's responses, and take your time. Building a relationship during the sales process is very much like building any relationship in your life. In fact, the same rules apply in sales as in any human interaction. Imagine, for example, a man and a woman on a first date. They sit down for dinner in a nice restaurant, the waiter comes over and pours the water, and before the waiter even comes back with the menus, the man turns to the woman and says, "So, uh, I was thinking on the way over here that, uh, you know, if things go good here tonight, I mean, uh, if you like the food and, you know, you like me, maybe you and I, you know, could maybe get married and have a few kids. Maybe even a dog and a little house? What do you think?"

> IF IT'S GOOD FOR DATING,
> IT'S GOOD FOR SALES.

What she's going to think is that he is a stalker who spends too much time playing video games in his mommy's basement. The relationship is going nowhere. Even if the woman sits through the entire dinner (a.k.a. the sales presentation), she has already made her decision. Her defenses are up, and alarm bells are going off. Our little man friend is going to have a difficult time closing the deal. Perhaps the deal has already been closed in the woman's mind—and not in a good way. It seems our little friend is going to spend many more nights alone in his Star Trek pajamas.

In sales and in life, you've got to be cool. You've got to take your time and extend yourself emotionally. Ask questions, and take a genuine interest in the responses. If it's good for dating, it's good for sales. The same rules apply. Let's imagine another man and woman on their first date. The waiter comes over and pours the water. As the waiter walks away, the man turns to the woman and says, "So, what do you do for a living (*Occupation*)?"

She responds, "I am a designer."

The man digs a little deeper. "Really? How did you get into that line of work?"

Once she explains how she got into her profession, he asks, "So, what do you do with your time when you aren't working (*Recreation*)?"

And on it goes. Each time she answers, he stays engaged with direct eye contact and an occasional nod of the head. He is sincere and genuinely interested. He looks for opportunities to ask deeper questions. After the date, he takes her home. He calls a day or two later and says, "Hey, that was a lot of fun. Would you like to go out again?"

"Of course!" she exclaims.

They go out again, and before you know it, they're an item. Within a few months, they're inseparable, and so much of her stuff is at his place, they are practically living together. Six months go by. Then a year. But he never pops the question. What happens now? Most likely, she starts telling her friends, "I don't know what's wrong. Everything seems perfect, but he won't close the deal! He won't propose. He won't ask for the commitment!"

You see, sales is very much like any other relationship. If you rush things, you'll turn people off. You'll scare them. You'll come across as desperate and over-anxious. But if you take your time and build the relationship, there will come a point in time when asking for a commitment seems natural. It's even expected. You've got to sell the same way you found your spouse. So begin your sales process in the relationship-building phase by asking questions, staying focused and engaged, taking a genuine interest in your prospect's answers, and digging a little deeper when it's appropriate.

The bottom line is that most top producers *are* genuinely curious and interested in others. They ask questions—not to "act" interested but because they *are* genuinely interested in people and their stories. Allow the relationship and the sales process to move along naturally, and there will come a time when asking for the business will seem natural. Your prospect will even come to expect it. After all, that's what happens in relationships, doesn't it?

PEOPLE BUY FROM PEOPLE WHO LIKE THEM

If you've heard it once, you've heard it a thousand times. Sales is all about building relationships, and people buy from people they like. You've heard it and said it countless times because it's true.

But here is something you may not have considered: *People also buy from people who like them.* We spend a lot of time trying to get people to like us, but we often overlook the very important step of letting them know we like them.

Letting people know you like them is a simple process. Showing genuine interest in them, asking questions— sometimes it's just as simple as saying, "Wow, you are a really interesting person. What a great story!"

Another simple way to let people know you like them is to ask their advice about something. After all, you ask advice from people you like, trust, and respect.

Suppose you see a picture of a deep-sea fishing trip with your prospect proudly displaying her catch. You could simply ask her, "Wow, I've always wanted to go deep-sea fishing. If you were going to give one piece of advice to a first-timer, what would that be?"

Maybe your prospect has a picture of himself on a motorcycle. You could ask, "I've always been interested in learning to ride. If you had one piece of advice for someone like me, what would it be?"

You will be amazed at how generous people are with information about the things they enjoy. But more importantly, you are sending an important message to your prospect that you like and respect them.

MOVING ON FROM THE SMALL TALK

As we move on from the small talk in the sales process, it's time to take your prospect by the hand and start moving a little further down the sales hallway. Keep in mind that, depending on your product, service, and sales cycle, you might be walking all the way down the sales hallway on the first visit, or you may have to spend several preliminary meetings just to set up the actual sales presentation. You might be walking down the hallway with one decision maker, or you might be walking down the hallway with a committee of decision makers.

Either way, the same rules apply. Your responsibility is to proactively address any and all potential objections before the prospect raises them, and close the escape routes. All of this is done to give you the opportunity to hold the prospect accountable at the end. Remember: Public declarations dictate future actions.

Keep in mind that your prospect has been down the sales hallway before. In many cases, it may not have been a good experience. He might have been lied to and misled by others. He is on high alert and has a healthy dose of skepticism. Your job is to transcend all the obstacles and succeed in the face of these challenges.

After the initial small talk about them, it's your turn to start talking about you and your company. Since risk is the single biggest factor in the decision-making process, I recommend tackling it head-on. It's the first door you should close. Your prospect is not likely to say, "Hey, there is a high degree of risk in us making the wrong decision, so could you please address why there is little or no risk in trusting your company?" You must be proactive. They won't say it, but in one form or another, it is what they are thinking. Your job is to gradually shed some light on the risk monster and use your expertise to slay it. Once you've done that, you can turn out the light, close the door, and move on to the next issue.

STEP TWO: ADDRESS ANY PERCEIVED WEAKNESSES OF YOUR COMPANY, PRODUCT, OR SERVICE

Once the relationship building is in full swing, it's a good time to address any perceived weaknesses of your company. Whether your company has a reputation for being the most expensive, or your company is new, or your company is too small (or too big), take the wind out of your prospect's sails by addressing the issue honestly and positioning the perceived weakness as a strength.

Begin by briefly telling your company story. Highlight issues that are relevant and position any perceived weakness as a strength. For example, if your company is large, highlight your access to resources for service and warranty issues. If your company is small, highlight your personalized service. If your company is old, highlight your hundred-year history. If your company is new, highlight how you left the old company, because you found a better way to do things.

The point is to find your strength and highlight it. If you believe that being a new company may be an objection at the end of the hallway, bring it out now. Don't wait until it comes up at the end. If you do, it's too late.

Things might go something like this:

You: "Mr. Prospect, I'd like to share some information with you about my company. We are fortunate to be a very new company. I say that because with all the changes in technology, it's difficult for the old stalwarts to respond quickly. In fact, until recently I worked at one of the oldest providers in the industry. I left that firm because I discovered new ways to use technology to help clients improve productivity and profitability. There were just too many layers of bureaucracy to get these new ideas to market where I was. Would you agree that small and nimble is often an advantage in responding to changes in the marketplace?"

Prospect: "Yes. I suppose so."

Now, this is what I call a "duh" question, because there is only one answer. "Duh" questions can be very helpful to get your prospect's agreement to your narrative. Once I have the prospect's agreement, I am prepared if they later say, "Well, we have always done business with ABC company, because they have been around a long time." If that happens, I can say, "Well, I certainly appreciate that, Mr. Prospect. But *earlier you said* that our ability to quickly respond to changes in the marketplace was actually an advantage over older, larger companies. Did anything happen to make you change your mind?"

This is a classic example of how you can leverage the Consistency Principle to close more business. You successfully got your prospect to make a public declaration that being new is an advantage. In this example, the prospect is more inclined to take action consistent with his previous declaration, which is to buy from you despite your company being new. Public declarations dictate future actions. The key is giving thought to what might come up at the end and addressing it proactively. You know what your weaknesses are, so you should prepare for them. Don't wait for your prospect to bring up that you are a new company. Any situation or characteristic can be positioned as an advantage with a little thought and preparation.

OUR BEST YEAR EVER

Here's another example. By 2007, about two and a half years after I opened my heating and air-conditioning company, we had generated over $7,000,000 in revenue out of a relatively small market of about 140,000 single-family homes. The good old boys who had dominated the market for decades were none too happy.

So in the spring of 2007, I was summoned to appear before the building department's mechanical committee that governed my license to install HVAC systems in the county. When I appeared before the committee, I realized that the members of this committee were also our direct competitors, whom we had taken to the woodshed over the previous thirty months. No conflict here.

In a nutshell, the members of the committee had decided that the community would be better served if the likes of me did not have a contractor's license. Never mind the thousands of satisfied customers and zero complaints of any kind. They were moved by their civic duty to protect the community from people like me. Touching, isn't it?

After the initial meeting, I hired a prominent attorney who quickly resolved the issue in our favor, as we had done nothing wrong. Nevertheless, during the weeks following the initial meeting, a local newspaper reporter was tipped off to the threat I posed to the community. (I imagined the clandestine meeting in a dimly-lit parking garage, where the dutiful reporter was given the explosive information by a mystery man known only as "Sore Throat.")

A few days later, the headline of our local newspaper read "Rebuilt Life in the Balance" (Google it for some entertaining reading). Along with the front-page article was an old mug shot of Yours Truly. Inside the paper was a *full-page* article outlining my entire life history. The exposure brought a sense of calm across the community. Families were safe. The public could relax, knowing the county building department was at their side.

WHATEVER! And get this: Over the next two years, our sales team would walk into sales appointments to find copies of my criminal record from the article that had been left by our competitors. It was a tough nut to crack for our sales team.

Nevertheless, we handled it the way we should all handle any potential weakness that may come between us and earning a prospect's business. During the initial stages of our sales presentation, whether or not the prospect brought up the newspaper article, our salesmen would say, "I'd like to tell you a story about the man who started our company. It's the ultimate story of redemption and overcoming adversity to achieve success . . ."

They would then go on to position my story in full context as a strength. As a result, we had our best year ever and doubled our sales in 2007. The moral of the story is that you cannot allow your competitors or marketplace gossip to tell your story. *You must proactively position any potential weakness (whether perceived or actual) before the prospect or your competitors bring it up.*

This strategy is just as important for large companies as it is for small ones. For example, we recently developed a customized sales presentation kit for a Fortune 500 company with annual revenues in excess of $30 billion. While this company is a household name and one of the strongest brands in any industry, they often struggled to win new customers, simply because customers perceived that changing providers was too much trouble, in spite of their superior service.

To address this "escape route" head-on, I simply

introduced a consistency anchor in the form of two questions the sales team would ask when presenting to the operations team of a prospective customer. After sharing two videos that demonstrated how the company partnered with other customers to help grow their companies, the sales professional was trained to ask these questions:

Question #1:

"Ms. Prospect, after viewing these two videos, would you agree that it is important to choose a service provider who is as committed to growing your company as much as they are interested in growing their own company?"

To which the prospect would respond, "Well yeah, I guess so." (Duh!)

Then Question #2:

"Ms. Prospect, would you agree that if my company could offer you a service that would help you grow your company and improve your overall operational effectiveness, it would be worth any short-term inconvenience of changing service providers?

To which she would respond: "Yeah. Sure." (Again, duh!)

Once the prospect makes these public declarations, they are far more likely to make a final decision that is consistent with what they have agreed to. Remember what I've stressed: It's key to set the consistency anchor *before* any attempt to close. Once you get near the close, you are unlikely to earn any concessions.

You must think about your prospect's objections and any perceived weaknesses and proactively close the escape-route doors before your prospect brings them up.

If you have a particular perceived weakness that you are struggling to overcome, join me each week on my online show, where I can help you develop a specific series of questions to get your prospects to agree that the perceived weakness is actually a strength. Visit www.WeldonLong.com to learn how to access the show.

STEP THREE: DISCUSS HOW YOUR COMPANY'S GUARANTEES ARE DESIGNED TO MINIMIZE RISK, AND THEN SHARE YOUR SIGNATURE STORY

Now, it's time to use your company's guarantees and signature story to demonstrate how your company minimizes or eliminates the risk of making the wrong purchasing decision. Remember, this will be different for each company depending on what risk-reversal guarantees your company may or may not offer. If your company offers a "satisfaction guarantee," you will use that. If your company offers no assurance to customers whatsoever, you will leverage your personal reputation and commitment to minimize the risk.

As I take risk head-on, I will also shine some light on the competitive-bids monster in the closet just in case my prospect is considering getting multiple proposals/bids. I want the prospect to realize that there is no risk in doing business with my company, and I want to use third-party verification from previous customers to prove it. I also want to have the prospect rethink the need to get competitive proposals.

The conversation might go like this:

You: "Ms. Prospect, in addition to our ability to quickly respond to changes in the marketplace, I'd like to tell you about the cornerstone of my company. It's our service-commitment guarantee. What this really says is that if you trust my company with this purchase and you are not happy with the quality or service that we deliver, we will move heaven and earth to ensure the situation is resolved to your satisfaction."

You: "You see, Ms. Prospect, we believe the risk of this decision should not be yours. We put the risk on our shoulders, which is right where it belongs, don't you agree?"

Prospect: "Sure. I suppose it should be your problem, not ours."

You: "I agree. You know if you buy a flashlight at Hardware Depot and it doesn't work or you just don't like it, you can return it. Why should it be any different in our business?"

Prospect: "I guess it shouldn't be."

You: "I'd like to share something with you that demonstrates what this guarantee means in the real world. Here is a letter from Mrs. Jones that outlines what happened when we dropped the ball on our service. You can see right here that we refunded her 50 percent of the cost of the service and reimbursed her for the inconvenience and aggravation. You can also see that she was very glad that she chose to trust us, because although we are human and make mistakes now and then, we put the responsibility of righting the wrong on our shoulders. We didn't make our problem into her problem."

You: "Ms. Prospect, how do you suppose Mrs. Jones felt when we stepped up to the plate and honored our service commitment to her?"

Prospect: "I'm sure she was very happy."

You: "Absolutely, she was. Here is another letter I'd like to share with you from Mr. Smith. You can see here that there was no problem with Mr. Smith's product; he just had a short-term issue with his cash flow, and we were able to modify the terms of his payment schedule to make it all work. Pretty awesome, isn't it? How do you suppose Mr. Smith felt when we stepped up to the plate for him?"

Prospect: "I am sure he appreciated it."

You: "I agree. Ms. Prospect, have you ever had a bad experience with service from a provider like ours?"

Prospect: "Oh yeah. Once, we couldn't get delivery on time, and it cost us a fortune. I was ready to strangle someone."

You: "What if that had been our company, and with one phone call, you knew we would step up to the plate and take responsibility for the mistake?"

Prospect: "That would have been amazing."

You: "Well, Ms. Prospect, that's the kind of service guarantee I am talking about here. There is no one in the industry more committed to our customers than our company."

The combination of your guarantee(s) and your signature stories creates a very powerful tool that demonstrates your high character and, therefore, that you are worthy of the prospect's trust.

Once you have discussed your guarantees and signature stories, you can move on to the next step.

STEP FOUR: ASK THE PROSPECT ABOUT THEIR PREVIOUS EXPERIENCES WITH GETTING MULTIPLE BIDS/ PROPOSALS, AND DISCUSS THE "THREE-BID MYTH"

In this step, the objective is to explore the prospect's previous experiences with getting multiple bids in an effort to illustrate the "three-bid myth," which shows that getting multiple bids rarely protects customers. Your prospect doesn't need the three bids. What they need is YOU.

You: "Let me ask you this, Ms. Prospect. Are you considering getting multiple proposals for this project?"

Prospect: "Oh yes. We always do."

You: "I completely understand. Is that how you found the provider that left you in a bind?"

Prospect: "Well, as a matter of fact, it is."

You: "It's amazing how that happens. Sometimes we talk to several different companies and still make the wrong decision, don't we?"

Prospect: "Unfortunately, yes. The company that we had the delivery problem with was the fourth company we interviewed."

You: "You know it seems like back in the day when your parents and my parents got three bids, they usually got three sets of truth. Do you think that's true today?"

Prospect: "Unfortunately not."

You: "I agree. In fact, these days we call it the "three-bid myth." Folks get multiple bids, because they want to feel protected. But our experience has shown that what people really need is one company that will take care of them when the chips are down—not three bids from companies who will say anything to get your hard-earned money."

STEP FIVE: ASK POWER QUESTION #1 TO CLOSE THE "I NEED MULTI-PROPOSALS" DOOR

By now you have made your point and are prepared to ask the first Power Question, which will help you close the "I need multi-proposals" door.

You: "Let me ask you this, Ms. Prospect. If on one hand you had the option of getting multiple proposals from multiple companies who might tell you anything to get your money, and on the other hand you had one company that would treat you the way we treated Mrs. Jones and Mr. Smith, which would you prefer?"

Prospect: "Well, the company that treated their customers the way they ought to be treated."

You: "I agree."

Here are a couple things worth noting. First of all, the word *prefer* is very important. If I say, "Which of those companies would you *buy* from?" I am likely to get a very defensive response. It's too soon in the relationship to be discussing buying. I am just having a casual conversation about preferences.

Second, I am not saying that from that point on your

prospects will never seek competitive offers again. What I am saying is that by having your prospect state that she doesn't necessarily need multiple competitive offers, *she is more likely to act in a manner consistent with that statement.* Remember: Public declarations dictate future actions.

Additionally, keep in mind that you are only beginning the process of chipping away at the prospect's fear and skepticism. You still have a lot of work to do and you will continue chipping away throughout the process. You must remain patient.

Finally, here's what you can say if you get down to the end of the sales hallway and your prospect stalls:

Prospect: "OK, that sounds good, but we have two other companies to talk with about this project."

You: "I see. Well, earlier you said if you had to choose between multiple companies who might say anything and a reliable company like ours, you would prefer a company like ours. Did something change during our time together?"

I will discuss where to take this conversation in the book's final chapter. Right now, I am trying to stress that you must lay the groundwork or you will be toast at the end. By considering the objections that may arise at the end and preparing yourself with questions and your signature story, you are paving the way to a much more productive conversation at the end of the sales hallway.

PERSONAL GUARANTEES

Because your company may not have a risk-reversal guarantee, I will modify the previous example using the sales professional's *personal* guarantee. It's a very simple process to leverage your personal integrity to accomplish the same result, and it eliminates the "my company doesn't have good guarantees so I can't do this" excuse. I simply shift the burden of responsibly from my company to myself.

> *You*: "Ms. Prospect, in addition to our ability to quickly respond to changes in the marketplace, I'd like to tell you about the cornerstone of my company. This is my personal "heaven and earth" guarantee. What this really says is that if you trust my company with this purchase and you are not happy with the quality or service that we deliver, I will personally move heaven and earth to resolve any issue to your satisfaction. You see, Ms. Prospect, I believe the risk of this decision should not be yours. I put the risk on my shoulders, which is right where it belongs, don't you agree?"
>
> *Prospect*: "Sure. I suppose it should be your problem, not ours."
>
> *You*: "I agree. You know if you buy a flashlight at Hardware Depot and it doesn't work or you just don't like it, it doesn't take an act of Congress to resolve it. Why should it be any different in our business?"
>
> *Prospect*: "I guess it shouldn't be."

You: "I'd like to share something with you that demonstrates what this guarantee means in the real world. This is a letter from Mrs. Jones that outlines what happened when we dropped the ball on our service. You can see here that I personally did whatever was necessary to resolve the issue to her satisfaction. You can also see that she was very glad that she chose to trust me, because although we are human and make mistakes now and then, we put the responsibility of righting the wrong on our own shoulders. We didn't turn our problem into her problem. Ms. Prospect, how do you suppose Mrs. Jones felt when we stepped up to the plate and honored our service commitment to her?"

Prospect: "I'm sure she was very happy."

You: "Absolutely, she was. Here is another letter I'd like to share with you from Mr. Smith. You can see here that there was no problem with Mr. Smith's product; he just had a short-term issue with his cash flow, and I stepped in to resolve it to his satisfaction. Pretty awesome, isn't it? How do you suppose Mr. Smith felt when we stepped up to the plate for him?"

Prospect: "I am sure he appreciated it."

You: "I agree. Ms. Prospect, have you ever had a bad experience with service from a provider like ours?"

Prospect: "Oh yeah. Once, we couldn't get delivery on

time, and it cost us a fortune. I was ready to strangle someone."

You: "What would it have been like if that had been our company and with one phone call, you knew I would have stepped up to the plate and taken responsibility for the mistake?"

Prospect: "That would have been amazing."

You: "Well, Ms. Prospect, that's the kind of service I am talking about here. There is no one in the industry more committed to our customers than I am. Let me ask you this, Ms. Prospect. Are you considering getting multiple proposals for this project?"

Prospect: "Oh yes. We always do."

You: "I completely understand. Is that how you found the provider that left you in a bind?"

Prospect: "Well, as a matter of fact it is."

You: "It's amazing how that happens. Sometimes we talk to several different companies and still make the wrong decision, don't we?"

Prospect: "Unfortunately, yes."

You: "I'm not sure, but I think that's because people will come in here and tell you anything to get your business."

Prospect: "Sad but true."

You: "Let me ask you this, Ms. Prospect. If on one hand you had the option of getting multiple proposals from multiple companies who might tell you anything to get your money, and on the other hand you had one company that would treat you the way I treated Mrs. Jones and Mr. Smith, which one would you prefer?"

Prospect: "Well, the company that treated their customers the way they ought to be treated."

You: "I agree."

You can see how simple it is to replace a company guarantee with your personal guarantee. You just need to be willing to serve your customers like they have never been served and then get letters from your customers to use as third-party verification.

DEALING WITH CONTRARIANS

Of course, you will occasionally come across the contrarian prospect who may refuse to make any concessions about previous bad experiences with other providers. If that happens, I can still move forward and close the door. Here is an example:

You: "Ms. Prospect, have you ever had a bad experience with service from a provider like ours?"

Prospect: "Not really. I've always taken the time to make the right decision."

You: "I see. Well, if you did ever have a problem with a provider, would it be useful to know that with one phone call we would step up to the plate and take responsibility for the mistake?"

Prospect: "That would be great."

You: "Well, Ms. Prospect, that's the kind of service guarantee I am talking about here. There is no one in the industry more committed to our customers than our company. Let me ask you this, Ms. Prospect. Are you considering getting multiple proposals for this project?"

Prospect: "Oh yes. We always do."

You: "Have you ever known a person who spent the time and effort to get multiple bids or proposals and then still had a serious problem with the provider they chose?"

Prospect: "No. Not really."

You: "Well, you are very fortunate. I speak with people in your position every day, and almost everyone has had problems with providers. You know, it seems like back in the day when your parents and my parents got three bids, they usually got three sets of the truth. Do you think that's true today?"

Prospect: "Yes. I think all salespeople are honest with their customers."

You: "Despite your good experiences, would you agree there are companies out there that might take advantage of customers?" (Duh!)

Prospect: "Well, I am sure there are." (It's very hard even for contrarians and skeptics to disagree with Duh! Questions).

You: (Power Question #1) "Let me ask you this, Ms. Prospect. If on one hand you had the option of getting multiple proposals from multiple companies who might tell you anything to get your money, and on the other hand you had one company that would treat you the way we treated Mrs. Jones and Mr. Smith, which one would you prefer?"

Prospect: "Well, the company that treated their customers the way they ought to be treated."

You: "I agree."

Occasionally, you will come across people who will not even make the smallest of concessions. They will refuse to agree with anything you say or ask. In that case, you can only do your best. Make your best presentation, and accept that all you can do is the best you can do.

Also, keep in mind that if you are currently closing four out of ten, that means that you are losing six out of ten.

You are looking for one or two out of the six you are losing that will be persuaded by this strategy. Stay focused on the opportunities where building trust and using consistency will be effective.

. . .

Although every presentation will be a little different, once you have completed the first phase of Relationship Building, you should have accomplished five things.

1. Engaged in traditional relationship building conversations (asking questions, showing genuine interest, etc.) and shared basic information about your company

2. Addressed any perceived weaknesses of your company or product or service

3. Discussed how your company's guarantees are designed to minimize risk and shared your signature story (demonstrated high character)

4. Asked the prospect about their previous experiences with getting multiple bids/proposals and discussed the "three-bid myth"

5. Asked Power Question #1 to close the multi-proposal door (consistency anchor)

Once you have accomplished those objectives, you are ready to continue building the relationship and move on to taking the price issue head-on.

CHAPTER 7

RELATIONSHIP BUILDING (PART 2)— BUILD TRUST, AND CLOSE THE "I NEED A CHEAPER PRICE" DOOR

In this chapter, you will learn how to build trust by using third-party experts to show your company meets or exceeds the highest industry standards.

Additionally, you will ask Power Question #2 and have your prospect make a public declaration that price is not the most important consideration in the purchasing decision. This closes the "I need a cheaper price" door.

Key Trust-Building Objective: Demonstrate high competency by using third-party experts to show your company meets or exceeds the highest industry standards.

Key Consistency Anchor: Ask Power Question #2, and close the price door.

Here is a quick outline of the conversation in step two of Relationship Building:

· Discuss industry experts and how your company meets and/or exceeds industry standards (demonstrate high competence).

· Ask Power Question #2, and have your prospect make a public declaration that price is not the most important factor in the purchasing decision (set consistency anchor).

After your initial assault on risk and competitive proposals, it's time to take a look at the "price monster" behind the next door. Keep in mind, whether or not your prospect brings up price, he is already thinking about it.

Pretending the price monster isn't there will not make it go away. You must prepare yourself now for the inevitable price conversation that is going to come up at the end. If you are not prepared when it comes up, you'll be in a very weak position. If you prepare for it early on in the sales process, you'll be in a strong position to maintain your margins.

THIRD-PARTY INDUSTRY EXPERTS

The first step in demonstrating your company's high competence and closing the price door is finding third-party industry experts who outline the most important factors when purchasing whatever it is you sell. All you have to do is search the Internet for "Things to consider when purchasing (insert your product or service here)." Watch how many articles come up published by reliable third-party experts and trade/industry associations. Make sure to find the perfect article that accomplishes two points:

1. The article outlines industry or trade recommendations on what factors should be considered when purchasing that particular product or service.

2. The article demonstrates that price is not the most important factor in the purchasing decision.

LIFE INSURANCE EXAMPLE

To illustrate, I am going to see how long it takes to find expert third-party support on what I should consider when purchasing life insurance and that supports my contention that price should not be the most important factor. A quick search of "most important things to consider when buying life insurance" turned up nearly two million articles in .62 seconds. Within another five seconds, I had found an awesome article from an industry trade organization. The article listed ten important things to know before purchasing life insurance. Price was number five.

Now, let me show you how easily I can use the article to demonstrate high competency and set a consistency anchor that price is not the most important factor in the purchasing decision—a fact that will come in very handy when price (premiums) come up at the end of the sales presentation. Remember, I have just completed my preliminary relationship-building activities and was successful in getting my prospects to declare that they would prefer my company over multiple proposals—after hearing and reading my signature story.

Me: "Mr. and Mrs. Prospect, I am sure that as you consider this life insurance investment, one of the factors that will impact your decision is the monthly premiums. Is that fair to say?"

Prospect: "Absolutely!"

Me: "I understand completely. I'd like to share an article with you that outlines some of the other things you might consider. This is from an industry trade group, and they outline some pretty important things. We like to use industry experts, because that's your assurance that we do things by the book."

At that point, simply read down the list of the things people should consider and then continue.

Me: "Now, as we evaluate your life insurance needs, these are all things we should discuss to make sure you are making the right decision for you and your family. Does it give you confidence in this process that we are relying on outside experts to make sure we get it right?"

Prospect: "Sure."

Me: "Great, before we get started with evaluating your life insurance needs, I wanted to point out that one of the things you said was important in making your decision is number five—the premiums. I don't know about you, but I was a little surprised to see premiums listed at number five."

Then, I go right into Power Question #2: "Let me ask you this: Would you agree or disagree with the experts that there are other factors as important, perhaps even more important, than a low premium?"

Prospect: "Well, yeah, I guess."

At this point, I have accomplished a lot. I have demonstrated high competency by using an industry expert as my guide in the process, and I have found a way for my prospect to make a critical public declaration that price is not the most important factor in the decision. I don't want to get too far ahead of myself here with closing, but let's think about my response now if my prospect objects to the premium at the end of the presentation.

All I have to do is remind them of their previous statement and say, "I understand the premium is a little higher than you expected, but earlier you said that you agreed that there are other factors more important than the premium. Has that changed in our time together?"

Prospect: "Uh. Well, no."

Me: "Well great! With your permission, I'll go ahead and start the paperwork."

Remember, under the Consistency Principle, your prospect will be inclined to take action consistent with their previous declarations, which is to consider other factors beyond the premium. Something else I have accomplished is the creation of an expectation that I am not going to be the cheapest solution. I don't want to go into the closing with my prospect expecting me to be cheap.

Sometimes when I ask Power Question #2 ("Let me ask you this, would you agree or disagree with the experts that there are other factors as important, perhaps even more important, than a low premium?"), the prospect will respond with, "Well, uh, you guys must be expensive."

When that happens, I simply respond by saying, "Actually, given our superior quality and service, we find that we are very competitive. So would you agree there are other factors more important than a low premium?"

Either way, I get the public declaration I need.

Just think about where you are in the sales process at this point. Before you met with your prospects, they were telling each other, "We are getting three bids! We are getting a cheap price!" Yet, within fifteen minutes, they have made completely opposite public declarations: that they would prefer your company over multiple proposals and that price is not the most important factor in their purchasing decision.

Those two things alone will completely change the dynamic of your sales presentation and will very likely change your zip code. Remember, if you don't persuade them to make public declarations that are consistent with buying from you, you will have allowed their previous public declarations to each other to drive their actions at the end.

NEW WINDOW EXAMPLE

Here are a couple of additional examples to show how easy it is to find expert third-party articles to support your argument. If you need more help, join me on my weekly show where I can help find the articles and help you craft the questions you need.

When I searched "things to consider when purchasing

windows," it took less than a nanosecond for Google to give me this powerful piece of expert third-party support from *Consumer Reports*: "Even the best windows won't deliver the look, comfort, or savings you expect if they're installed poorly."

This will serve as the perfect support for my contention that price should be a secondary consideration when shopping for windows. The article also outlined other factors that homeowners should consider when making the purchasing decision on new windows. Price is never the most important.

With that information, I could have a conversation that sounds like this:

Me: "Mr. Prospect, after reading this article, would you agree or disagree that proper installation of your windows is as important, perhaps even more important, than a cheap price?"

Prospect: "Sure. I would agree."

Me: "Let me ask you this question, Mr. Prospect, if another company came in and offered to install your windows for a cheaper price, but failed to install them properly, would he have really saved you any money in the long run?"

Prospect: "I guess not."

Me: "I agree."

I think you get the picture.

HEALTH INSURANCE EXAMPLE

My search of "most important things to consider when buying healthcare" immediately revealed a useful article that listed important considerations when considering health insurance in the following order:

1. How much health insurance do you need?

2. What type is the best policy?

3. Do you qualify for coverage?

4. Where do you get the best price?

5. How strong is the insurer?

Obviously, this is very important information to have on hand as we demonstrate our competency relating to our evaluation of the prospect's health insurance needs. It also helps us communicate the fact that price should not be the most critical determinant when choosing an insurance plan. As you can see, price is number four.

Here is an example of how I could use the information to get my prospect to make a public declaration that price is not the most important factor when choosing an insurance plan.

Me: "Ms. Prospect, when you evaluate health insurance plans, will price be one of the factors you'll consider when making a decision?"

Prospect: "Absolutely."

Me: "I agree. Now, when you are talking about price, are you talking about the down and dirtiest price with no regard for quality? Or are you talking about a fair price with great quality and service—a great value?"

Prospect: "Yeah. A great value."

Me: "That's what I thought you meant. I'd like to share with you some information from the experts. This is an article from an industry website that outlines some of the most important issues to consider when purchasing life insurance. I like to use the experts, because they typically give good objective advice."

I then describe the article and read the list of important issues to consider:

1. How much life insurance do you need?
2. What type is the best policy?
3. Do you qualify for coverage?
4. Where do you get the best price?
5. How strong is the insurer?

Me: "Sounds like a pretty good list of things to consider. Why do you suppose they list 'price' as only one of five issues on the list?"

Prospect: "I'm not sure. I guess because they are all important."

Me: "Absolutely. Would you agree or disagree that some of these other issues are as important, perhaps even more important, than price?"

Prospect: "Sure. I would agree."

Me: "Let me ask you this question, Mr. Prospect: If another agent came in and offered you a policy for a cheaper price, but it was not the right policy and he represented a weak insurer, would he have really saved you any money in the long run?"

Prospect: "I guess not."

Me: "I agree."

Now, does this mean your prospect will never consider price again? Of course not. Price is always an issue. But we are only beginning the process of chipping away at price and laying the groundwork to be prepared when price comes up at the end of the sales hallway. When it does, you'll be prepared to say, "Mr. Prospect, earlier you said that a cheaper provider was not necessarily the best provider. Has that changed over the last sixty minutes?"

Prospect: "I guess not."

Me: "Great, let's start the paperwork!"

REALTOR EXAMPLE

Here is an example I have used with hundreds of realtors to help them win more listings.

A quick search of "things to consider when choosing a realtor" revealed a little gem from a major news magazine's website that listed these five important questions to ask prospective realtors:

1. How long have you been in the business?
2. What geographic areas and types of properties do you handle?
3. How will you communicate with me?
4. Can you share references?
5. What will it cost to sell my property?

With this information I could have a conversation with a prospective client that goes like this:

Me: "So, Mr. Prospect, I am sure as you evaluate realtors, one of the things you will consider is the commission. Is that fair to say?"

Prospect: "Absolutely. I know all those signs on bus benches aren't cheap!"

Me: "That's funny, Mr. Prospect. At any rate, I'd like to share an article with you from this magazine that outlines some of the things you might consider when choosing a realtor."

At that point, go through the article and explain how you excel in all five areas. (By the way, if one of the things to consider is a weakness for you, simply search for a different article. For example, if you are a brand new realtor, you might use an article that doesn't list the length of an agent's career as one of the things to consider.)

Once you have covered all the points, simply say, "You know, Mr. Prospect, I was surprised that commission was the least important of these factors. I mean even if a realtor charged a smaller commission but did nothing to market your property, it probably wouldn't be in your best interest, would it?"

Prospect: "I guess not."

Me: "Let me ask you this: Would you agree with this publication that there are factors to consider that are as important, maybe even more important, than the commission?"

Prospect: "Well, I guess. But you must be one of those 6 percent realtors."

Me: "Honestly, we have found that given our ability to quickly market and sell your home at a price you will love, we are very competitive. Would you agree that maybe that's the most important thing—selling your home at a great price?"

Prospect: "Well yes. Of course."

Me: "I agree."

Now, let's fast forward to the end of the meeting if the prospect questions your commission.

Me: "So, Mr. Prospect, will you trust me with your listing?"

Prospect: "Well, yes, I trust you, but your commission is higher than some other realtors' commissions."

Me: "I understand, but earlier you mentioned that the most important factor is selling your home at a great price. Has that changed?

Prospect: "Of course not."

Me: "Great. With your permission, I'll start the paperwork."

Boom! Another listing in the bag. Drop the mic.

THIRD-PARTY RESULTS
FOR VARIOUS PROFESSIONS:

Financial Planner—*Forbes* magazine
(Fees: # 3)

1. Education and experience
2. Certifications
3. Fees and conflicts of interest

4. Standard of care

https://www.forbes.com/sites/rogerma/2017/01/04/5-things-to-look-for-when-picking-a-financial-advisor/#6cbda91fc44e

Mortgage Broker—RealtyTimes.com
(Closing costs: # 7)

1. Loan amount
2. Mortgage features
3. Mortgage rate
4. Monthly payment
5. Term
6. Locking
7. Closing costs

https://realtytimes.com/consumeradvice/mortgageadvice/item/26213-20130923-choosing-a-mortgage-understand-these-7-factors

Automobiles—Edmunds.com
(Sale Price: # 5)

1. Research vehicles and features.
2. Get preapproved for a loan.
3. Plan your trade-in.
4. Locate and test-drive the car.
5. Check sale price and warranties.
6. Review the deal and dealer financing.
7. Close the deal.
8. Take delivery

https://www.edmunds.com/car-buying/10-steps-to-buying-a-new-car.html

Residential Contractor Services—PopularMechanics.com

(Price not even mentioned)

1. Make sure the contractor is licensed to work in your area, bonded and insured.
2. Pick a contractor who specializes in your project type.
3. Have a detailed contract in place before any work begins.
4. Find out who's performing the work.
5. Give contractor guidelines for working in or around your home.
6. Know what your responsibilities are.
7. Ask about a mechanic's lien.
8. Look at work samples.
9. Think locally.

*https://www.popularmechanics.com/home/interior-projects/how-to/
g648/10-tips-for-hiring-a-contractor/*

I can hear the conversation now: "Mr. and Mrs. Homeowner, on this list of ten things to consider when choosing a contractor, price isn't even listed. Would you agree with *Popular Mechanics* that there are a variety of factors that are as important, maybe even more important, than a cheap price?"

"Uh, yeah, I guess."

Public declarations dictate future actions.

Will it work ten out of ten times? No. But it will work with many of the opportunities you are losing, and that's all that matters.

Regardless of what your product and service is, you can easily find third-party experts who cite factors more important than price. You just have to take a few minutes and practice the conversation.

At the end of the day, we all know that it never really makes sense to buy the cheapest of anything. Your prospect knows it too; you just have to have an honest conversation with them about price so they will acknowledge that.

Think about it: When does it make sense to buy the cheapest of anything? I have asked that question to thousands of sales professionals and I've never received a good answer. I once had someone say, "Gasoline! I always buy the cheapest gasoline!" I guess that's close, but I promise you I'm not putting the cheapest gasoline in my Ferrari! You're probably not putting the cheapest gas in your car, either.

Your prospects don't have the cheapest car or the cheapest television or the cheapest cell phone. Don't let them mislead you into believing that THIS TIME (with your product and service) they are buying the cheapest solution.

It's not true. You know it, and they know it. You just need to have an honest conversation about price and get them to publicly declare that price is not the most important consideration in their purchasing decision.

CHAPTER 8

INVESTIGATE THE PROBLEM— BUILD TRUST, AND CLOSE THE "I NEED TO THINK ABOUT IT" DOOR

In this chapter, you will learn how to build trust by conducting a comprehensive and systematic diagnosis to investigate your prospect's problem.

Additionally, you will ask Power Question #3 and have your prospect make a public declaration that they can let you know *today* whether or not you are a good fit for them. This closes the "I need to think about it" door.

Key trust-building objective: Demonstrate high competency by conducting a comprehensive and systematic diagnosis to investigate your prospect's problems.

Key consistency anchor: Ask Power Question #3, and close the "I want to think about it" door.

Here is a quick outline of the conversation during the investigation of your prospect's problems:

· Identify your prospect's problems (trust-building activity).

· Identify negative emotions associated with the problems.

· Gain prospect's permission to offer solutions to the problems.

· Ask Power Question #3, and have your prospect make a public declaration that they can reach a yes or no decision.

The most basic definition of marketing is to find a need and satisfy it. It's the same thing in sales; while sometimes the process seems complicated, it isn't. It's a simple process of identifying the prospect's problems and offering solutions to remedy them.

When consumers are evaluating whether or not they will purchase something, they are in essence dissatisfied with a particular condition or situation, and they are willing to do something to improve that condition or situation. The divide between where they are and where they would like to be often creates negative emotions. Your job as a sales professional is to identify the problems and the negative emotions associated with the problems and to offer solutions to both.

Up to this point, we have spent time analyzing and preparing for objections that will likely come up at the end of the sales hallway, which is really all about being prepared for the close. In this section, we will prepare ourselves for the inevitable "I want to think about it" (and countless variations of that objection), and we will also work through the process of learning how to identify your prospect's problems, uncovering additional problems that your prospect may be ignoring, and identifying emotions that can be used to influence the prospect's final decision.

The traditional sales process includes finding out what your prospect "needs" and/or "wants." The assumption is that, if you can accurately identify what your prospect wants and needs and address those issues, you will have a better chance to earn the prospect's business. This is only partially accurate. Consistency Selling is more complex than offering some "thing" to solve a prospect's problems. To truly become a top producer in sales, you must also uncover the emotion that is fueling the need and/or want and offer a solution to the emotional "dis-ease."

The challenge, as you will see, is that oftentimes the prospect himself is unaware of the emotion driving his purchasing decision. Thus, you must not only identify it, but you must also communicate it accurately to your prospect.

You can make a living in sales by finding what people want and need. You can make a fortune by understanding the emotions that are driving the purchasing decision. But that will require a deeper level of questioning and a higher degree of listening and professionalism.

Therefore, as we work through this stage of the process, we will seek to identify wants and needs *and the emotions underlying the wants and needs.* We will seek to identify the emotional discomfort and how we might resolve it.

If I had to credit just one sales concept that helped me go from a homeless shelter to earning millions of dollars in the sales profession, it would be my ability to identify emotional drivers, communicate those to my prospects, and offer solutions to resolve the emotional discomfort related to their want/need/problem.

Therefore, the series of questions you will ask your prospect will be designed to uncover their needs and wants but also to reveal the emotions driving the purchasing decision. You can create an entirely new set of questions to use in your sales process, but generally I find that sales professionals already have a series of questions they use when presenting to clients. The ideal strategy would be to take the information from this section and use it to create a few new questions to add to your own sales process.

UNCOVER THE EMOTIONAL DRIVERS

Before we get into the specific line of questioning you will use, let's discuss some of the challenges facing sales professionals when they attempt to identify the prospect's problems and emotional discomfort.

When consumers are evaluating the purchase of anything, there is an internal balancing act that permeates the decision-making process. Imagine a set of scales in the prospect's mind. One side is the prospect's money. The other side is the prospect's problem.

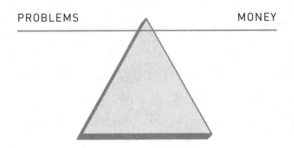

PROBLEMS   MONEY

As the prospect considers his options for solving his problem, he is evaluating the "value" of the solution versus the "value" of his money. If the prospect ultimately decides that your solution to his problem is more valuable than his money, he will exchange his money for your solution, and you will make the sale. If the prospect ultimately decides that your solution is less valuable than his money, he will not exchange his money for your solution, and you will not make the sale.

Demonstrating that the solution is more valuable than the prospect's money can sometimes be very difficult, especially when the purchase pits the rational versus the emotional mind. A perfect example is life insurance. While there are many who can't afford life insurance, there are millions of others who can afford it but simply choose to spend their money on solving other problems. These consumers have decided that the value of minimizing their family's financial risk in the event of a future crisis (rational) is not as valuable as how the money *feels* in their pocket today (emotional).

This is a perfectly legitimate decision for consumers to make. It's a balancing act, and it is the sales professional's responsibility to demonstrate that his/her solution is more valuable than the prospect's money. If we cannot articulate the value of our solution, we shouldn't complain that the prospect makes what we believe to be the wrong decision and keeps his money.

Examples of this dilemma abound. Look at your neighbor's house that needs painting. You may not be able to understand how he lives with his home looking that way. It's simple: The value of a freshly painted house is less than the value of his money. Look at your friend's car with the smashed door. Perhaps it would make you crazy to drive a dented car, but clearly your friend values his cash more than he values not having to enter his car through the passenger side. It's all a matter of priorities and perceived value. Maybe no one has adequately articulated the value of a painted house or a repaired door. Maybe the value is simply not there.

Consider this: Most everyone reading this book has an automobile. You have in effect made the decision that the solution to your transportation problem is more valuable than whatever money you spent on your car. But what if the least expensive car on the market was $100,000? Would you still be driving a car? Or would you be taking a bus, bicycle, or horse to work? We all have our balancing act, don't we? While you may value the solution to your transportation more than the $30,000 your car cost, you may not value the solution more than $100,000. It's all a personal choice.

In the sales process, the answer to this conundrum is very simple. All you have to do is demonstrate to your prospect that your solution to his problem is more valuable than his money. And to accomplish this, all you have to do is expand his problem to such an overwhelming degree that his money seems small in proportion. Make his problem seem gigantic, and his money will seem insignificant. When the problem is huge, the solution is significantly more valuable. But human nature is a fickle companion, and our challenge is human nature.

It seems we humans have a tendency to minimize our problems. We convince ourselves that the odds of needing life insurance are small. We convince ourselves that the damage to our unpainted home won't be that serious. We convince ourselves that we don't really look stupid or are endangering ourselves by getting in and out of our car from the passenger side.

Additionally, humans tend to focus only on the problem at hand. We often intentionally ignore or unintentionally overlook other problems, because instinctively we know that solving more problems costs more money. Have you ever taken your car in for one problem and intentionally ignored another, because you knew it would cost more to get both problems fixed? Suppose you take your car to the garage to get the starter fixed and the mechanic says, "You know, your brakes sound odd. Would you like me to take a look at them while I have the car here?"

"No," you respond. "Just fix the starter. The brakes are fine. I think they are just wet from last week's rain." Problems cost money to fix. It's as simple as that.

DEFY HUMAN NATURE

So your job is to defy your prospect's human nature and demonstrate that his problem is huge and the solution you can offer is far more valuable than money. The problem must be bigger, much bigger, than the money. When the problem gets bigger, the solution gets more valuable.

PROBLEMS   MONEY

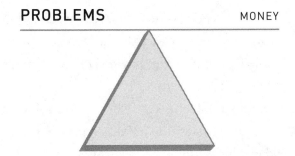

To make the problem bigger, we will need to do a little probing with questions and identify additional problems the prospect may be ignoring or overlooking. We'll want to bring to his attention any emotional problems that can be solved as well. The combination of unknown and ignored problems and emotional issues below the surface can be used to illustrate the significance of the problem and, therefore, the value of the solution.

Use questions to identify problems you can solve for your prospect.

As you work through the questioning process, you will simply ask your prospect about their problem and how they feel about it. During that process, you will probe into issues they may be intentionally ignoring or unintentionally overlooking to assist you in making their problem take on a greater importance—greater than the value of their money.

Occasionally, a sales professional will balk at the prospect of identifying additional problems the prospect may have out of a misguided notion that they are being nosy or pushy. Some sales professionals may believe their job is to solve the problem they are there to address—not probe into other problems the prospect has not raised. If you think it is not your responsibility to identify and solve ignored and overlooked problems, consider this: Imagine you go to your primary physician to address a problem with your gall bladder. Your doctor expertly diagnoses your problem, recommends a treatment, and solves your problem.

Wonderful. Good doctor.

Two weeks later, you suffer a heart attack. While narrowly escaping death, you are resting in ICU when you see your gall bladder doctor who is attending to her other patients.

"Hey, doc!" you exclaim. "How you doing?"

"Much better than you, it appears," she says. "What happened?"

"Well, two weeks after I saw you for my gall bladder, I had a serious heart attack. Damn near killed me!"

"I am not at all surprised," she says. "I thought your heart was going to explode the day I did your physical."

"What?" you inquire. *"You knew I was going to have a heart attack?"*

"Well, of course, I knew. Your heart was arrhythmic, and your blood pressure was through the roof. A first-year medical student could have seen you were about to have a heart attack. Frankly, I was surprised you made it out of my office."

"Are you kidding me?" you demand. "YOU KNEW I WAS GOING TO HAVE A HEART ATTACK? Why didn't you say something? What kind of quack are you? Are you a doctor or the grim reaper?"

"Hey," she calmly responds, "you came to see me about your gall bladder, not your heart attack."

How much confidence would you have in the doctor? Probably not very much. You see, we expect the professionals in our lives who are fixing one problem to tell us about any others they may encounter. We can decide if we want to fix the other problem or not, but we don't want them to take that option away from us.

So do you still think it's a professional's job to address only the problems brought to their attention?

Take this one step further, and ask yourself how you would feel if your doctor said, "Well, I was going to tell you about the heart attack, but I got to thinking about how much heart surgery or treatment you could really afford."

How would you feel if your doctor was qualifying your budget before recommending treatment that could save your life?

Yet isn't it true that many sales professionals fail to recommend solutions because they have prejudged the prospect's budget? Don't be that person.

VIEW YOURSELF AS A PROFESSIONAL

If you want to be a top income earner in sales, you have to view yourself as a professional. You should see yourself as every bit the professional as your doctor, and it is your doctor's professional responsibility to diagnose problems and recommend solutions to health issues, whether or not you bring them up. It would be malpractice for your physician to ignore a serious problem, and it is likewise professional malfeasance for you to willfully ignore problems that you have the talents and ability to solve for your customers.

This is *not* high pressure. It is *high service.*

Your job is to diagnose problems and recommend solutions. Period.

Remember Joe the Concrete Guy? Was Joe a pushy snake oil salesman? No. Joe was just really good at the *process* of identifying problems and offering solutions. I doubt that Joe gave a rat's rear end whether or not I spent more money with him. His focus was on how a seemingly smart and successful guy could be such a bonehead to park a motorcycle trailer in the rocks and dirt.

DON'T TAKE REJECTION PERSONALLY

This is a good spot to address another issue that afflicts some sales professionals: taking rejection personally. To illustrate the absurdity of taking rejection personally, let's take another look at your relationship with your physician.

Suppose you knew you had a heart condition, and your doctor recommended that you avoid fried, fatty foods and lose a few pounds. An hour after your doctor visit you are sitting at McDonald's (ironically located in the hospital lobby), wolfing down a double cheeseburger and a "biggie size" order of French fries. You look up with special sauce dripping down your chin to see your doctor watching you. You sheepishly hang your head and take another bite of your double cheeseburger.

Ask yourself this question: Does your doctor take it personally that you did not accept her recommendation? Does she get her feelings hurt that you chose a different option? Of course not. *Her job is to diagnose problems and recommend solutions.* She is not personally invested in your decision. In fact, she *expects* that not everyone will accept her recommendations.

And so it should be for sales professionals. Accept your professional responsibility to diagnose problems and recommend solutions. Don't take it personally if your prospect (patient) chooses to go in a different direction.

Ask predetermined questions to identify your prospect's problems, identify any negative emotions associated with the problem, and gain the prospect's permission to offer solutions to the problems.

As you craft your questions for this process, think about all the different types of problems your product and/or service can solve. Often, prospects do not realize that the company that can solve "problem A" can also solve "problem B." Remember that your prospect may ignore or overlook problems that you could solve for them. This is especially true if they don't even know you could solve those other problems.

To keep things in context, consider where we are in the

process. You have just completed outlining your company story and using third-party verification to show why there is little or no risk in trusting your company and why multiple proposals may not be in the prospect's best interest. You have also established that your prospect is not making the decision based solely on a cheap price.

Keep in mind the importance of asking questions in such a way that your prospect agrees with your narrative. Remember, only your prospect's public declarations will dictate his future actions—your public declarations will have little or no impact on what your prospect eventually does. As the old adage goes, "Telling is not selling."

QUESTIONS THAT REVEAL EMOTIONS

Your questions should be scripted out and start with surface-level conversational questions and gradually move to more pointed ones. I typically begin the questioning process by saying, "I'd like to get your opinion on a few things. Is that okay?" Don't start by saying, "I'd like to ask you a ton of questions. Is that okay?" No one likes to be interrogated (trust me on this). But everyone loves to give their opinion. The questions you asked during the Relationship-Building section were more of a personal nature. The questions you ask now are designed to understand problems and reveal the emotions driving the purchasing decision.

Let's begin with a very simple example. Suppose you are selling financial services products. Your company sells a variety of insurance, retirement, and investment products that can solve many of your customers' problems.

Use a questionnaire to diagnose your prospect's problems. If you already have one, you can use what you have. There is no point in reinventing the wheel. The key is to use the questionnaire in a fashion that will reveal useful information. Don't zip through it with a "checklist" mentality. It's not so much about what questions you ask—it's about how you ask them. The key questions will be unique for each industry, but they are not likely to change from prospect to prospect within a particular industry. Ask the questions in such a way that you can learn the following two things:

1. What is the problem, and how does that make your prospect feel?

2. Will the prospect give you permission to offer solutions to the problem?

In the financial services example, the questionnaire should begin with very basic information, such as verifying name, address, contact information, and basic information about the prospect's family. These are good surface-level conversational questions.

Here is an example of how to structure the questioning process:

Sales Professional: "So, Mr. Prospect, let's discuss your financial goals and see if we can help you get there. I'd like to get your opinion about where you are now and where you'd like to be in three to five years in the following areas."

Prospect: "Okay, fire when ready."

Sales Professional: "What is one of your most important financial goals?"

Prospect: "Getting a new car." (Your prospect may be minimizing his financial planning problems.)

Sales Professional: "Great. So what kind of car are you driving now?" (What is the situation now?)

Prospect: "A 1973 Gremlin."

Sales Professional: "So you want to be driving something different in five years?"

Prospect: "Well, the car is a classic, but I wouldn't mind driving something more reliable."

Sales Professional: "So the car breaks down from time to time. Can you give me an example?"

Prospect: "Yeah. Last winter, I was taking little Susie to school, and it broke down in a snowstorm."

Sales Professional: "Wow. How did you feel about that?" (How does that make the prospect feel?)

Prospect: "I was pretty frustrated. A little embarrassed, too."

You can always tell when you've discovered emotions that will drive the purchasing decision, because your prospect will use emotive terms—in this case "frustrated" and "embarrassed."

Keep in mind your goal here is simply to identify the problem (not having enough money to buy a new car) and the emotions that will drive the purchasing process (frustration and embarrassment). Don't worry about how you'll use this information right now. At this point it's about gathering the information.

Sales Professional: "If you could buy a super reliable new car in five years, what car would that be?" (What could the situation be?)

Prospect: "A Land Rover all-wheel drive."

Sales Professional: "How cool would that feel on a snowy morning?" (How would that make the prospect feel?)

Prospect: "I don't know about cool, but it would feel safe." (I will accept "safe" as an emotive term.)

Sales Professional: "Got it. Is that something I should keep in mind when I design your financial strategy? After all, we are talking about three dollars a day over five years." (Getting the prospect's permission to offer a solution to his problem of not being able to afford safe and reliable transportation for little Susie.)

Prospect: "Yeah, I guess so. That's less than a Starbucks a day."

Over the course of about two minutes, you've identified the problem (no money for new car), and you have found the emotions that will drive the purchase, which can be used during the closing sequence.

Also, by asking the last question, you have gotten your prospect's permission to offer him a solution to this problem. Effectively, he is asking you to offer him a product to help him afford a new car, which might be a product designed to help him save for a new car or maybe a product to consolidate credit card debt so he can afford the new car. You will figure out the best solutions later.

At this point we simply want to identify the problems and emotions associated with the problem and gain permission to offer a solution later in the process.

KEEP THE QUESTIONS SIMPLE

It's very important to keep this questioning process simple. Just find out where your prospect is and where he would like to be, and then figure out how you can help him get there. Remember: Diagnose and recommend.

As you move through the questions, repeat the process with various areas of the prospect's financial life:

retirement, mortgage payoff, support for aging parents. Each time you find a problem, simply ask the prospect, "Is that something I should keep in mind when I design your solution?" By the time you are finished, you will have identified four or five problems (some previously ignored or overlooked), and your prospect will have asked you to recommend several different financial products to solve them.

Let's take a look at another line of questioning that illustrates how you can uncover problems the prospect is ignoring or overlooking. Each of these provides additional problems, for which you can offer solutions. Furthermore, each problem you uncover increases the size of the problem and, therefore, the value of the solution.

Sales Professional: "So let's talk about your kids' future. Looks like you've got plenty of time before paying for college. What are your plans for that?"

Prospect: "Well, I haven't thought much about it. It's a long time off."

Sales Professional: "So right now you have saved nothing for their college?" (What is the situation now?)

Prospect: "I haven't been able to."

Sales Professional: "Does that worry you?" (How does that make the prospect feel?)

Prospect: "Yeah."

Sales Professional: "Suppose you could wave the 'magic college wand.' What would you have happen for your kids' college?" (What could the situation be?)

Prospect: "Harvard Business School."

Sales Professional: "Wow. How would that make you feel?" (How would that make the prospect feel?)

Prospect: "Like Dad of the Year."

Sales Professional: "You know, if you start saving now, it wouldn't have to be a fortune every month. Sounds like that's something I should take into consideration when I design your plan."

Prospect: "I guess so."

Your prospect has now asked you to recommend a college savings product for his kids (in addition to a plan to save for his new car). He has also given you the emotional driver ("being Dad of the Year") to use in your closing sequence.

REMEMBER THAT YOU KNOW A LOT MORE THAN YOUR PROSPECTS ABOUT HOW YOUR PRODUCT AND SERVICE CAN SOLVE PROBLEMS FOR THEM.

Amazingly, only moments ago, he was completely overlooking or ignoring this problem, yet now he knows about it and has asked you to solve it for him. The value of your solution is rapidly exceeding the value of his money. The more problems you identify, the more likely he is to be willing to exchange his money for your solutions.

Remember that you know a lot more than your prospects about how your product and service can solve problems for them. It's your job to ask questions to understand the prospect's initial problem. But you must investigate further and uncover additional problems your prospect may not realize you can solve for them. As you uncover the problems and emotions, get permission to offer solutions. You will gain priceless information about where your prospect is and where he would like to be. You will also gather priceless information about the emotions that will drive the purchasing decision in the closing sequence.

ASK POWER QUESTION #3

Once you have concluded the questioning, wrap things up by setting a consistency anchor and closing the "I need to think about it" door. Keep in mind where you are in the process. Depending on how much time you spent in the Relationship-Building and Investigate-the-Problems stages, you may have already been with your prospect for forty-five to ninety minutes. Everyone should feel comfortable at this point.

Sales Professional: "Mr. Prospect, before we go on, I'd

like to ask you a question. Have you ever had the misfortune of dealing with a pushy salesman?"

Prospect: "Oh yeah. When I bought a new ABC widget."

Sales Professional: "What was that like for you?"

Prospect: "It was terrible. The guy would not leave me alone."

Sales Professional: "I understand. Well, I've got some great news for you. I am not a pushy salesman. I am a financial services professional. This is how I make my living. It's how I feed my family and serve my community. I will not be the guy hounding you for a week to buy something from me.

Here's how I prefer to do business: I'd like to take all the time you need today for me to answer all your questions and explain things so you can make an informed purchasing decision. There is no rush. You are my only priority.

All I ask is this: Once I answer all your questions, design the perfect financial plan and, of course, make it all fit within your monthly budget, all I ask is that you let me know one way or the other whether or not I am a good fit for your family. And by the way, 'no' is a perfectly acceptable answer. Fair enough?"

Prospect: "You mean make a decision tonight?"

Sales Professional: "Just let me know whether you think I am a good fit for you and your family. I am not going to hound you. It doesn't sound as though you liked it when the ABC widget salesman did that. As I said, keep in mind that 'no' is a perfectly acceptable answer."

Prospect: "OK. That seems reasonable."

Now, of course, things won't always go according to this scripted plan, but keep in mind, you are looking for a few of the prospects you are currently losing. If my prospect won't agree to let me know whether or not I am a good fit, I always like to rephrase the question and ask again. I call this the "One Dollar Scenario."

Prospect: "Well, no, I can't let you know tonight. This is going to be a big decision."

Sales Professional: "I understand. Let me ask you this: What are you looking for in a financial services plan?"

Prospect: "Something that's safe. A company that's been around a long time. Someone who is willing to explain things in a way I can understand. And some-one I can trust."

Sales Professional: "Well, that's a pretty good list. Suppose I could demonstrate to you that we are the best in the business in all these categories. I'm not saying I can do that, but just suppose I could. If you believed that we were number one in every one of these categories, and, for one dollar, I could help you reach your financial goals in a reasonable amount of time, all I am asking is that you let me know whether or not I am a good fit for your family.

Prospect: "OK, but the answer might be no!"

Sales Professional: "I understand. That's not a problem."

SELLING DOESN'T HAVE TO BE A CONSTANT STRUGGLE

By this point, you have laid the groundwork, gathered a ton of valuable information, and are ready to propose a solution to the prospect's problems and proceed with your closing sequence. You are performing your professional duties like a champ, and you will have the opportunity to bring this sales presentation to a conclusion—one way or the other—and move on to new opportunities.

Selling doesn't have to be a constant struggle. All you have to do is make new friends, diagnose, and recommend.

Let's take a look at another example. This time, we'll look at a B2B scenario that involves selling CRM software and a longer sales cycle. Keep in mind where we are in the process—we've already moved beyond the chitchat phase and closed some escape-route doors.

Sales Professional: "Mr. Prospect, what I'd like to do now is get your opinion on some things."

Prospect: "OK. I've got a lot of those."

Sales Professional: "How long have you been using CRM software?"

Prospect: "About five years."

Sales Professional: "And what were you using before that?"

Prospect: "We were small, and we were new, so we just kind of kept track of things with notes and a few spreadsheets."

Sales Professional: "Boy, you've come a long way since then. How long have you been using your current provider?"

Prospect: "The whole five years. They were our first."

Sales Professional: "I see. How have things been going with them?"

Prospect: "Pretty good, actually. I'm just curious about new options and technology that may be available."

Sales Professional: "I see. Are there any specific things you've heard about that got your attention?"

Prospect: "Well, I've heard that some of the new CRM programs will integrate with certain phone systems, so we could have customer information and history as soon as we answer the call."

Sales Professional: "What happens when your customers call now?" (What is the situation now?)

Prospect: "We transfer the call and then tell the sales rep who is calling. Our rep will then pull up the information before he takes the call."

Sales Professional: "What is it about that scenario that you don't like?"

Prospect: "It just takes too long. We are all about service. Sometimes it can take a minute or more to get the call to the rep and have the account information pulled up."

Sales Professional: "Has that caused any issues with customers?"

Prospect: "Occasionally. Our customers are busy, too. They want to get in and get out. Sometimes ninety seconds on hold can seem like a lifetime."

Sales Professional: "Could you tell me about a specific example?"

Prospect: "Yeah. A few months ago, one of our oldest customers was on hold for a couple of minutes and kind of dropped a hint that he wasn't happy. When I heard about it, I gave him a call. He said it wasn't a big deal but then joked about us not using technology like the rest of the civilized world. Sometimes people joke about things when they are trying to make a point."

Sales Professional: "How did it feel when he made the joke?" (How does that make the prospect feel?)

Prospect: "It wasn't very funny. I felt like we were letting technology get out ahead of us."

Sales Professional: "Would you describe your feeling as frustrated?"

Prospect: "Maybe a little."

Sales Professional: "How would it feel if you had a system where your receptionist could greet your clients by name when she answered the phone, and then instantaneously transfer the call plus customer information and history to the sales rep?" (What could the situation be, and how would that make the prospect feel?)

Prospect: "Like a rock star."

Sales Professional: "Sounds like I should keep that in mind when I design your system."

Prospect: "Definitely."

The prospect has now asked you to recommend a solution to the problem, which might include a new phone system in addition to the CRM software. At this point, it would be a great idea to probe into any additional potential problems you can address that the prospect may be ignoring or overlooking.

Sales Professional: "So how is your reporting with respect to measuring sales performance?"

Prospect: "Oh, it's fine. We have a system that measures close ratio, average sale, and average revenue per lead."

Sales Professional: "Could you share with me how it works?"

Prospect: "Sure. We have the sales reps keep a log of their inbound leads and sales. We then take their sales numbers and do the math."

Sales Professional: "So the numbers are only as reliable as the information put in, right?"

Prospect: "Well, yeah. Garbage in, garbage out."

Sales Professional: "Have you ever had a situation where a sales rep disqualifies a lead and doesn't count it in his numbers?" (What is the situation now?)

Prospect: "Sometimes that happens. And it makes me crazy. I've told them I have to have accurate numbers to run this business!"

Sales Professional: "Do they always do as they are told?"

Prospect: "C'mon. They are salespeople."

Sales Professional: "What's your reaction when they do

it after you've told them not to?" (How does that make the prospect feel?)

Prospect: "It's not pretty. Imagine a human volcano."

Sales Professional: "You know, many of our CRM solutions automatically measure sales performance. There is no playing with the numbers. What would that be like for you?" (What could the situation be, and how would that make the prospect feel?)

Prospect: "That would be amazing. I could actually rely on my sales numbers."

Sales Professional: "Is that something I should keep in mind when I put together your proposal?"

Prospect: "Absolutely."

I wish I could say this process was more complicated. (Actually, I don't wish that. I am happy as a clam that it's simple.) All you need to do is find out where your prospect is, where they would like to be, and probe into the areas they haven't thought about. Beyond that, make a note of the emotions you can use to drive the purchasing decision.

With the questioning process finished, simply set the ground rules.

Sales Professional: "Mr. Prospect, before we go on, I'd

like to ask you a question. Have you ever had the misfortune of dealing with a pushy salesman?"

Prospect: "Oh yeah. When I bought the turbo-encabulator."

Sales Professional: "What was that like for you?"

Prospect: "It was terrible. The guy would not leave me alone."

Sales Professional: "I understand. Well, I've got some great news for you. I am not a pushy salesman. I am a CRM sales professional. This is how I make my living. It's how I feed my family and serve my community. I promise you that I will not be the guy hounding you to buy something from me.

Here's how I prefer to do business: I realize that you'll have a process to go through internally before you pull the trigger. What I'd like to do today is take all the time you need for me to answer all your questions and explain things so you can make an informed purchasing decision. There is no rush. You are my only priority.

All I ask is this: Once I answer all your questions, design the perfect CRM solution, get the price right, and walk through the purchasing process, you let me know—one way or the other—whether or not I'm a good fit for your business. And by the way, 'no' is a perfectly acceptable answer. Fair enough?"

Prospect: "Sure. Sounds reasonable."

At this point, you have gathered useful information and set the ground rules to bring this process to a conclusion at the appropriate time. Of course, there are no guarantees, just the highest probability for success.

As you demonstrate how the prospect's problem is becoming bigger and more complex, your solution will become ever more valuable to the prospect. As the solution becomes more valuable, the prospect will become more likely to exchange his money for your solution.

You know the good news: This is a simple process. And you know the bad news: It's just a little easier not to follow it.

Once you've completed this step in the process, you will have identified numerous potential solutions to your prospect's problems, and you've gained his permission to offer solutions to those problems. You will have also identified the emotional drivers that will be of tremendous help during your closing sequence.

And, most importantly, you have gotten your prospect to publicly declare that he can let you know today whether or not you are a good fit, which will be enormously helpful if and when your prospect says, "I need to think about it" during the closing.

You are expertly navigating the hallway, and the endgame is in sight.

CHAPTER 9

SELL YOUR COMPANY AND SOLUTIONS—BUILD TRUST, AND SEAL THE "I NEED A CHEAPER PRICE" DOOR SHUT

In this chapter, you will learn how to build trust by presenting a compelling picture of your company and how to conduct a product/service demonstration to show that your company has the competency to expertly deliver the product and/or service.

Additionally, you will ask Power Questions #4, #5, and #6 and have your prospect make a public declaration that they do not want to sacrifice quality for a cheap price. This seals the "I need a cheaper price" door closed, and it permanently changes the price dynamic between you and your prospect.

Key Trust-Building Objective: Demonstrate high competency by presenting a compelling picture of your company and conduct a product/service demonstration to show that your company is trustworthy.

Key Consistency Anchor: Ask Power Questions #4, #5, and #6, and permanently change the price dynamic.

Here is a quick outline of that conversation:

· Present proof of your company's competency (trust-building activity).

· Use product/service demonstration to show that your company is trustworthy and competent (trust-building activity).

· Ask Power Questions #4, #5, and #6, and permanently change the price dynamic.

Once you've escorted your prospect down the sales hallway, closed a few doors, identified the problems, and discovered some of the emotions that will drive the purchasing decision, it's time to sell your company and its solutions. This is a simple process that involves demonstrating to your prospect why your products and/or service and your company are the best option to bridge the gap between where they are and where they would like to be.

This step is the heart of your sales presentation; it's where you'll present the quality and service your company provides. You will essentially outline your competitive advantages and superior quality and service. Keep in mind you will not make the formal offer (asking for the order) until the next step. In this step, you will seek to ensure all the doors are closed and demonstrate why your products, services, and company are awesome.

TIMING IS EVERYTHING

In my experience, it is best to perform this step only when you've reached the opportunity to close. In other words, if your meetings to this point have been to set up the opportunity to *present* to decision makers, don't perform this step until you have the opportunity to *close* with the decision makers.

The reason for this will become clear as we move through this step and deliver powerful information that will provide you with significant momentum going into your closing sequence. If you attempt to perform this step and then return to close later, you will deprive yourself of a powerful opportunity.

Additionally, once you have completed this step, your

prospect will have all the information he needs to make the purchasing decision. If you disengage after this step and without going through the final stage (Concluding the Call), your prospect will likely make the decision without you in the room.

> KEEP IN MIND THAT AT ITS CORE, SALES ARE A TRANSFERENCE OF EMOTION.

Keep in mind that at its core, sales are a transference of emotion. If you distance yourself from your prospect at this crucial moment (in the hope they will call you next Tuesday), the emotion will have dissipated or even disappeared. By the time you reach the elevator, the prospect will have forgotten your company's name. By the time you reach the parking garage, he will have forgotten your name. By the time you reach your office, he will have forgotten what makes you special. By the time Tuesday rolls around, you are just a price sitting on his desk.

The bottom line is this: *Do not attempt to sell your company and solutions unless and until you are in the appropriate situation to move seamlessly into your closing sequence with the appropriate decision makers.* If you perform this step without bringing the call to a conclusion, be prepared for a phone call, letter, or email announcing the prospect's decision to choose another company. Sometimes you won't even get that.

> NO MATTER HOW MUCH THE NON-DECISION-MAKER WANTS TO BUY FROM YOU, HE WILL BE ILL PREPARED TO SELL IT TO THE DECISION MAKER.

Occasionally, a sales professional will deliver the heart of his presentation without the decision maker present in the hopes that the non-decision-maker will sell the solution to the decision maker. If you are ever tempted to do this, keep in mind there is a great difference in knowing your product and service well enough to buy it and knowing it well enough to sell it. No matter how much the non-decision-maker wants to buy from you, he will be ill prepared to sell it to the decision maker.

PRESENT THE PROOF

Once you have made the decision that the opportunity to close is available to you, simply announce to your prospect that you have a little more information to share with him about your company's competency and that you will soon share a few solutions to his problems. This is especially important if you are about to close the deal in that initial sales call—what we call a "one-call close." If you have already spent an hour or so with your prospect, she may be wondering how much longer the presentation is going to take. So it's a good idea to let her know the end is in sight. Try saying something like this:

"Ms. Prospect, we are just about done here. I have a little more information to share with you about my company, and then I'll get to some options for a solution. Fair enough?"

If you have been with your prospect any length of time, they will appreciate knowing where they are in the process, and in many cases, you may visibly see your prospect relax, as they know you are nearing the end. At this point, you should be demonstrating why your company, product, and service provide the best option to solve the prospect's problems. One of the most effective ways to accomplish this is with stories about your company and your team.

At the end of each story be sure to ask a "duh" question—a question that has only one obvious answer. Their response to each "duh" question is simply another brick in the consistency wall, and consequently your prospect will be more likely to act in a manner consistent with her public declarations in the final step of closing. Again, there are no guarantees. You are just giving yourself the best probability for success.

Finally, this is the time to have any and all third-party verifications on hand to support your stories. Licenses, certifications, insurance, proof of workman's compensation, awards, and industry recognitions can all be helpful as you demonstrate your company's competitive advantages. If you are selling a product that includes any components that you can physically demonstrate, you will have an enormous edge when it comes to closing. Many products and services are considered "commodities" by consumers, and using a product demonstration can help to connect your prospect with your product.

Once you have made the decision that a closing opportunity awaits you and you have assembled all your third-party verifiers, it's time to get to work. Begin the conversation with any story you choose.

> *Sales Professional*: "Ms. Prospect, we are just about done here. I have a little more information to share with you about my company, and then I'll get to some options for a solution. Fair enough?"

> *Prospect*: "Great."

> *Sales Professional*: "I'd like to start by showing you this certification and industry award. The certification demonstrates that we have successfully completed ABC training in our industry, and this award reflects our outstanding performance in the industry. I'll never forget the day we won this. Everyone in our office was bouncing off the walls. In fact, Maria, the lady that you spoke to when you called our office, got so excited she tripped over a box and fell. Once she got over the shock of falling, she laughed hysterically until she cried. The award is a huge accomplishment and a reflection of our outstanding team.

> Do you think it's important to work with a company that can verify certification and has been recognized as a leader within its own industry?" (Duh!)

Prospect: "Of course."

Sales Professional: "Why do you say that?"

Prospect: "Well, it means you know what you are doing and are very good at it." (public declaration of your competency)

Sales Professional: "I agree."

With this line of questioning you have accomplished two things: You have tried to take your company out of the commodity category *and* draw an emotional connection between the prospect and your company with the "Maria" story. You have also gotten your prospect to publicly declare good things about your company, which may have an impact on her future actions in the next step. All it took was a "duh!" question and a simple follow-up of "Why do you say that?" You have essentially given your prospect the answer and then asked a question to have her repeat the answer to get the public declaration.

Let's take another example from the actual HVAC sales presentation I used in my company.

Sales Professional: "Mr. Homeowner, I'd like to share a document with you from an organization called NATE. That stands for North American Technician Excellence, which is an organization that certifies that our service technicians have achieved the highest level of training.

It's really the gold standard of technician excellence in our industry.

Unfortunately for all the HVAC owners out there, only a very small number of HVAC technicians have qualified for this recognition. The good news is that 100 percent of my technicians have completed the training and certification. I remember once when a lady who had no heat in her home called us. It was freezing, and several companies had been out to try to fix her heating system to no avail. Finally, she called us, and we sent one of our NATE-certified guys out who fixed it in about fifteen minutes. Our guy felt so bad for her that he didn't even charge for the repair service.

Our guys are not just technically competent; they are good, decent guys. Is it important for you to have that kind of technician involved with the installation and service of your system?" (Duh!)

Prospect: "Well, yeah."

Sales Professional: "What makes you say that?"

Prospect: "So I know it's installed and serviced properly." (public declaration of your competency)

Sales Professional: "I couldn't agree more."

Stories are the best way to bring your company and your people to life and establish an emotional connection with your prospect. This is especially compelling if you were able to use third-party verification in the Relationship-Building phase to demonstrate that dealing with the right service provider is one of the most important considerations in the purchasing process. You are making it very easy for your prospect to say yes to you.

Here is another example I used to destroy my competition (without mentioning them by name!) and grow our heating and air-conditioning company to $20,000,000 in sales in 60 months.

Sales Professional: "Mr. Homeowner, this is a copy of our workman's compensation insurance. You'll notice the effective date is current, which is very important. It's important because it's expensive, and it's one of the things many contractors will cut when money gets tight. So anytime you have work done on your home, you must ensure your provider has valid insurance.

Now, you may be thinking this is not your problem, but imagine this scenario: A guy is up in your attic installing your system. Suddenly you hear a loud noise and someone screams in agony. Next thing you know, the installer is tearing through your house with a serious injury to his hand. In fact, from the fleeting glimpse you got, it looks like he may have lost a couple of fingers. These installations, after all, are not child's play—that's why workman's comp is so expensive in our industry.

Anyway, the guy goes to the hospital and is disabled for six months. He gets an attorney to collect on workman's comp, but the attorney soon finds out the contractor let the workman's comp expire to save a few bucks. Who do you think the attorney is coming after next?"

Prospect: "Me. The homeowner."

Sales Professional: "You better believe it. People will sue you over anything these days. So, can you see why it's so important that your contractor has valid workman's compensation insurance and can verify that for you?" (Duh!)

Prospect: "Absolutely."

Sales Professional: "Why is that?"

Prospect: "In case someone gets hurt. I don't want to be on the hook." (public declaration of your competency)

Sales Professional: "I don't blame you."

Your stories don't always have to be warm and fuzzy. Sometimes real-life situations can be serious, and there is nothing wrong with letting your prospect know it. With this story and series of questions, I have not only had the prospect make a public declaration, but also I've planted a seed of doubt. What do you suppose he is thinking about the other companies who failed to show proof of workman's compensation insurance?

Duh.

Let's take one more example. I have had the privilege of working with some of the largest network marketing companies in America. I am a huge fan of the network marketing industry, as it provides an affordable option for folks who are driven by a sense of entrepreneurship and self-reliance. The men and woman in this industry tend to be among the most driven and optimistic people I have ever met. I love the industry, and I love the people in the industry.

One of the biggest challenges facing network marketing professionals is recruiting others to help grow their business. Overcoming this challenge can become easier when network marketing professionals try to make friends, diagnose, and recommend. Doing this alleviates some of the pressure of recruiting, while highlighting the benefits of their business opportunity in this stage. Here is an example:

> *Network Marketing Professional:* "You know, Mr. Prospect, one of the most amazing things about my company is how easy they make it for others to succeed. I remember when I started in this business, I was a nervous wreck! I didn't know how to approach people or what to say. But I studied the training material and got very comfortable very quickly. In fact, the process I am taking you through right now was spelled out for me, step-by-step. I learned it in a couple of days. Pretty much anyone can do it—you just have to keep an

attitude of 'Make friends, diagnose, and recommend,' without getting too hung up on the outcome.

Getting involved with the opportunity was the best decision I ever made. Do you think it's important that a company provides a training program that's easy to follow so you can get up and running without a lot of hassle?" (Duh!)

Prospect: "Well, yes."

Network Marketing Professional: "Why do you say that?"

Prospect: "So I can get started quickly and get over my nervousness." (public declaration)

Network Marketing Professional: "I agree with you 100 percent!"

You can see that telling stories and asking a few simple questions can assist you in demonstrating to your prospect that your company is well suited to fill the gap between where they are and where they would like to be. Not only do you say it in a story, but by asking questions, you can have your prospect saying it too.

The bottom line is that you already know why your company is best suited to solve your prospect's banking, insurance, real estate, window, prepaid funeral, automobile, or printing problem. Your job is to prove it to them and get them to publicly declare what you already know.

DEMONSTRATE TRUSTWORTHINESS

In many situations, a sales professional can beef up their sales presentation with an actual product demonstration. Anything you can come up with that is a tangible, physical representation of your product quality is extremely valuable to prove why your product is the best solution for the prospect's problem. Once you've done the demonstration, you can ask Power Questions #4, #5, and #6 to permanently change the price dynamic.

One of the biggest challenges I faced when building a heating and air-conditioning company was elevating our products and services out of the commodity category where most homeowners put heating and air-conditioning systems. In the minds of many homeowners, all heating and air-conditioning systems were identical, regardless of who they purchase it from. They viewed their HVAC system the way they viewed their refrigerator. In their minds, it didn't matter where they bought the system, because the installation was as simple as wheeling in the furnace and plugging it in. Therefore, most purchasing decisions were made on price and price alone.

Of course, the reality is far different. HVAC systems are complex mechanical systems that must be designed and installed by skilled professionals, and our entire sales process was geared to show that to homeowners.

To visually and physically show our competitive advantage, we used a product demonstration to drive the point home to our potential customers. The process was simple.

We gathered together as many components to an HVAC system as we could. We collected valves, refrigerant lines, flexible gas lines, electronic controls, filters, and even the little rubber footers we put underneath the furnace on the basement floor. We put these items together in a "product demonstration kit," which we used to show how a proper installation should be performed and why we were likely to be more expensive than our competitors. We would conclude the product demonstration with Power Questions #4, #5 and #6, which slammed the door shut once and for all on the price monster.

Piece by piece, component by component, we demonstrated our competency to homeowners by showing them what each item did and why it was so important to a proper installation. With each item, we informed the homeowner that many companies would skip certain steps to get to a cheaper price. We would then assign a value to each component and let the homeowner hold each item in their hands. The conversation would go something like this:

Sales Professional: "Mr. Homeowner, this is component ABC, which is a filter that will extend the life of your system many years by eliminating contaminants in the refrigerant. This little item costs us about $50 and adds an hour or so in labor costs to the job. It may not seem important, but if it's not installed and your system lasts half as long as it should, I don't think you'd be happy.

Now, if I were looking to be the cheapest guy, this

would be one of the steps I could skip, because you would never know until it was too late. But I am not trying to be the cheapest guy. I will never skip steps that will compromise your system." (At that point, I would hand the item to the homeowner.)

We would repeat this process for six or seven components—each time assigning value to the item and handing it to the homeowner. After a few minutes, we would have all the items sitting there on the kitchen table. The homeowner had a clear vision of hundreds of dollars of value, and, perhaps, for the first time, he truly understood what's involved in the installation process and why our company was better than others.

At the end of the product demonstration with all the parts on the table, we asked three Power Questions, which completely changed the price dynamic.

Sales Professional: "Mr. Homeowner, when you consider how important all these components are to the life of your system and the safety of your family, why do you suppose so many companies skip them?" (Power Question #4)

Prospect: "To save time and money."

Sales Professional: "Exactly. So let me ask you this: If a company came in and offered to do a system for $500 or $1,000 less than I do, but he skipped these steps and as a result his system lasted half as long as mine, would he have really saved you any money?" (Power Question #5)

Prospect: "I guess not."

Sales Professional: "I agree. You know, Mr. Homeowner, in a few minutes I am going to share some system options and prices with you. Sometimes when people see how much high quality really costs, homeowners will want to know if I can drop my price and do the job cheaper." (Often the prospect will display a sheepish grin, because that's exactly what he is thinking.)

Now that you know what I would have to do to drop my price, is that something you are going to ask me to do?" (Power Question #6)

(POW! Checkmate!)

Prospect: "I guess not."

Does this mean a prospect will never ask for a cheaper price? Of course not. They are human, and asking for a cheaper price is in our DNA. But what it will do is eliminate some of your prospect's conviction about getting a cheaper price. More importantly, it gives you enormous leverage when the inevitable price monster rears its ugly head at the end of the sales hallway.

This process can be used for any product—whether it's a car, a tire, a copy machine, sporting goods, printing and binding services, vacuum cleaners, electronic equipment, or furniture. Just take a look at your product, and get your hands on the components that go into it. Most manufacturers will provide retailers and resellers components that can be used to demonstrate superior value and quality. All too often, sales professionals have these items and don't use them. Perhaps it seems like too much trouble? Think again!

Even if you are selling a service (and not a product), you can find your competitive advantage and show it to your prospects and end the demonstration with the same three questions.

Let's take an example of selling educational services:

Admissions Counselor: "Mr. Prospect, I'd like to share with you what goes into making a business degree from ABC College a superior degree. This is a textbook from Professor John Jones. Professor Jones is the leading expert in economics in the country, and we use his textbook for our economics courses. Does that cost us a little more than using textbooks from lesser-known economics authors? Probably. And while it may not seem like a big deal today, it will be when you are sitting across the interview table a few years from now.

Next, I'd like to show you a series of marketing videos we had produced by the leading marketing expert in the country. These videos are provided for you to enhance the scope of your marketing education. Were they cheap to produce? No. Would it have been cheaper for us to simply skip them? Absolutely, but we are not trying to provide the cheapest education in the country. We are trying to provide the very best."

You could repeat this process for as many small differentiators as you can imagine that would make your company stand out: Your building could be a competitive advantage, or your location, or your hours of operation. Anything you can use to show a competitive advantage.

Once you complete the demonstration ask the three questions:

Admissions Counselor: "Mr. Prospect, when you consider how important all these little things are to the value of your education, why do you suppose other schools skip them?"

Prospect: "I don't know. Maybe to make it cheaper?"

Admissions Counselor: "Exactly. Suppose another school offered an education for a little less money but cut corners in these areas, and you ended up with an inferior education. Would they really have saved you any money in the long run?"

Prospect: "I guess not."

Admissions Counselor: "In a few minutes, I am going to share tuition rates with you. Sometimes students will wonder why our tuition is slightly higher than other programs. Now that you understand the value of getting an education here, is that going to be a concern?"

Prospect: "I suppose not."

Does this mean your prospect will never consider a cheaper education? Of course not. But what it will do is get your prospect to think twice about getting a cheaper education. It's about improving your probabilities. There are no guarantees. Furthermore, whatever the impact on your prospect's future actions, it will give you powerful leverage when price comes up at the end of the sales hallway.

Once you have clearly demonstrated why your company is the best option to solve your prospect's problems and you've asked Power Questions #4, #5, and #6, you are just about finished with this step.

The last thing you have to do is explain the solutions you are going to recommend in the final step. If it is a financial product, take some time to explain it. If it is a hybrid car with super-duper fuel efficiency, explain how the technology works. If it is software to improve productivity, explain how it works.

KNOW YOUR SOLUTION

The bottom line is that at this point in the process, you should know exactly what solution you are going to recommend in your closing sequence. Make sure that you have fully explained the technology behind your recommendation before attempting to close. The last thing you want to happen during the closing sequence is for your prospect to get confused by the technology or complexity of your solution.

It's likely your prospect may have contacted you about one problem, but you may have identified additional problems during your questioning process. Be sure to explain how each solution would solve each problem before you attempt closing your prospect on each solution.

Let's suppose you are a financial services sales professional, and your prospect contacted you about a retirement plan. However, during your walk down the sales hallway, you identified other problems that your products will solve. Keep in mind that you are not closing at this point. You are only explaining. Also keep in mind that you may have numerous solutions that would solve the prospect's problems, but you are only going to explain the solution that you are going to recommend in the next step. REMEMBER: The confused mind says, "No!"

The conversation might sound like this:

Sales Professional: "Mr. Prospect, let's discuss a solution to your retirement problem. We have product ABC that will prepare you for retirement and make sure you can live the life you deserve after you've worked for so many years. Here is how the product works."

Go on to explain the details of how it works. Make sure you answer all the questions now. You don't want your prospect confused about the product when you enter your closing sequence in the final step.

> *Sales Professional*: During our conversation earlier, you mentioned that I should also keep little Joey's college tuition in mind when I design your financial strategy. There is a product called XYZ that will ensure that his college tuition and expenses are covered. Here's how it works . . .
>
> Finally, you suggested I consider a health insurance solution in the final plan as well. Here is product PQR, which is specifically designed with families like yours in mind. It works like this . . . "

You are explaining anything you are going to recommend at the end of the sales hallway. Will your prospect buy every solution you offer? I don't know. It doesn't even matter. Your job is to diagnose and recommend. It is your prospect's job to decide what he wants to buy. You do your job, and let the prospect do his.

Remember: It's the doctor's job to diagnose and recommend treatments. It's the patient's job to decide if he wants to follow the recommendation. Your doctor does not make the decision to recommend based on whether or not you will buy it. She makes her recommendation based on solving your health problems. That's her professional responsibility. It's your professional responsibility too. It's up to the patient/prospect to decide where to go from there.

Far too many sales professionals make the decision on

what to recommend based on what the *sales professional* thinks the prospect wants or can afford. This is a mistake and extremely presumptuous. It's the height of arrogance to make that decision for a prospect. There is plenty of work for sales professionals to do. There is no need to make important decisions for the prospects. That just adds to your workload.

LET'S CHANGE THIS DYNAMIC

Now that you have demonstrated why your company is best suited to solve your prospect's problems and explained the specific products and services to accomplish this, I recommend asking one final question before moving into your closing sequence.

Before I give you the question, think about this: What is usually the first thing that goes through a consumer's mind when they see the price of something? Think about the last time you purchased a television, or a boat, or a car. I have asked this question to thousands of sales professionals, and usually the answer is the same: "How can I get it cheaper?" It's what most consumers think when they see the price of *anything,* and it causes a lot of trouble for the sales professional—he is trying to close, and all the prospect can think about is how he can get the product cheaper.

So let's change this dynamic. Let's change it to reflect all the work you've done as you walked your prospect down the sales hallway. *Everything about you and the way you do business should create the expectation that you are not the cheapest option in town.*

The entire process of showing why your company is awesome and the care and quality that go into your products and services was designed to create the expectation that *you are going to cost more* than your competition. In fact, you solidified this expectation with your comments about "not being the cheapest company" in your product demonstration.

You did all of this so that you could change the dynamic at the end of the sales hallway. You did it all so the last thought going through your prospect's mind just before you go into your closing sequence is, "Man, I hope I can afford these guys."

To increase the probability (no guarantees) that your prospect is thinking this, you conclude this step with the following question:

Sales Professional: "So, Mr. Prospect, based on everything you have seen today about our company, our products and services, and our amazing people, is there any reason other than price you would not trust my company with this purchase?"

To which your prospect will say, "No way. If I can afford you guys, I am going with you."

He is also thinking to himself, "Man, I hope I can afford them."

The thing is this: You are probably *not* going to be much more expensive than your competition. *If you have successfully extended yourself emotionally and professionally to your prospect and demonstrated your superior quality, you will be worth an extra 10 or 20 percent.*

And price will be the ONLY issue at this point. You've built a very compelling wall of evidence that you are a great choice for your prospect. You've shown with third-party verification, customer testimonials, and your product and service demonstration that your company does things the right way and stands behind its customers 100 percent. Could there really be any doubt in your prospect's mind that you'll provide the highest quality product and service? Of course not. The only issue now is whether or not your prospect can afford you. And at this point, he is hoping he can.

I am always amazed at salespeople who are unwilling to build a strong relationship with their prospect, unwilling to confront objections proactively, and unwilling to demonstrate superior value. They rush down to the end of the hallway with all the doors behind them wide open, and then complain they can't sell because their prices are too high.

But you are different. You are willing to do the work so you can reap the reward.

At this point in the process, you are standing in front of the last door in the sales hallway—the door that leads to earning your prospect's business. You have earned the trust. You have built the relationship. You have proactively dealt with any objections while getting your prospect to make declarations that are consistent with buying from you. You have also demonstrated high character and high competency. As a result, you are ready to start closing. You have EARNED the right to start closing.

CHAPTER 10

CONCLUDE THE SALES OPPORTUNITY—LEVERAGE TRUST AND CONSISTENCY, AND ASK FOR THE ORDER

In this chapter, you will learn how to demonstrate high competency through making specific recommendations for solutions to solve the prospect's unique problems. You are the expert and should understand your prospect's problems and be able to customize solutions for them.

Additionally, you will ask Power Question #7 to leverage trust and the prospect's public declarations to bring the call to a conclusion by asking for the order.

Key Trust-Building Objective: Demonstrate high competency by making specific recommendations for solutions to solve the prospect's unique problems.

Key Consistency Anchor: Leverage the prospect's public declarations to bring the call to a conclusion.

Here is a quick outline of that conversation.

· Summarize the prospect's problems and make specific recommendations based on the prospect's problems and your expertise (trust-building activity).

· Make a formal and specific request for the order.

· Leverage trust and consistency to bring the sales opportunity to a conclusion.

I'm going to reference Zig Ziglar one last time: "If you can't close, you're gonna have skinny kids." I would add to that, "If you can't close, you'll never be more than an unpaid consultant."

You already know that the "C" in the R.I.S.C. model does not stand for "close." It stands for "conclude the sales call." You can't close every sales opportunity, but you can bring every sales call to a logical and reasonable conclusion.

Allow me to explain why *yes* is best, but *no* is a perfectly acceptable answer.

Your objective on every sales opportunity should be, whenever possible, to have your prospect reach a final and definitive decision about you and your company with you in front of them or on the phone. If you can accomplish this, most of the final decisions made in your presence will be yes. Yes is best, but no is a perfectly acceptable answer.

Don't get me wrong here. I am going to do *everything* in my power to close the deal, but I am also going to do *everything* in my power to remove the excuses, justifications, and objections and get a final decision with my prospect right in front of me—even if that final answer is no.

In my considerable experience, I've known many in the sales profession who prefer ambiguity to a definitive no. They believe that as long as there is not a definitive no, they still have hope that the customer may actually call back next Tuesday. They are afraid of the no. Well, my friends, in the immortal words of Red from my all-time favorite movie, *The Shawshank Redemption*, "Hope is a dangerous thing. Hope can drive a man insane."

I'll go a step further and say that in the sales profession, irrational hope can keep your kids skinny and ensure your employment as an unpaid consultant.

When you walk away from a sales opportunity without a definitive answer, human nature drives you to hope and believe the deal might come through if you just wait long enough for the prospect to talk himself into it. That's pure folly. It's simply not going to happen on a consistent basis. Might it happen on a rare occasion? Perhaps—but you will never build a career as a top producer on callbacks.

I remember once teaching a two-day sales event and making this point on the second day of the event. It was a Tuesday. During one of the breaks, a so-called sales professional came to me and said, "Guess what? I just got a callback for a deal. And today is Tuesday. What do you think about that?"

I looked into his eyes and said, "I think you are ruined for life. Good luck with all that. Enjoy your skinny kids." By the age of five or six, we all stop believing in Santa Claus, the Easter Bunny, and the Tooth Fairy. Yet I am amazed that there are countless salespeople at the age of forty, fifty, and sixty years old still believing in the pure, unmitigated fantasy that our prospect is going to call us back next Tuesday. Alas, denial ain't just a river in Egypt.

THREE REASONS YOU
NEED A DEFINITIVE ANSWER

· Subsequent calls suffer.

· Relationships weaken with time.

· Once the call is over, it's over.

There are three reasons why I believe it's a fatal blow to your income to leave sales opportunities without a definitive answer.

First of all, it's a major distraction on the calls immediately following the unresolved opportunity. Because it's so easy for humans to rationalize that an unresolved sales opportunity is going to magically become a yes, we don't focus and perform at our best on the next few calls. Our brain allows us to start counting phantom commissions, which removes the urgency and pressure to do well on the next few calls. When the prospect doesn't call back after a week and we finally accept yes is not going to happen, only then do we refocus on closing new business. By then, however, chances are we have squandered numerous leads and opportunities.

The second reason it's a bad idea to leave a call unresolved is because relationships only get weaker with the passage of time. Think about it: We all know that good relationships with our prospects are critical to our sales success and that people buy from people they like and trust. So when do you imagine your relationship is at its peak with your prospect? At the end of your brilliant presentation—or a few days later when your prospect has forgotten your name?

The relationship with your prospect will always be at its peak at the end of your sales presentation. The relationship NEVER gets stronger after you leave. NEVER.

So if you believe that relationships are important to

your sales results, it is imperative that you capitalize on the relationship when it's at its strongest and bring the call to a close. It is your absolute best chance to earn their business. When you combine the value of a strong relationship with your prospect's inability to say no directly to you, there is never a better probability of earning their business.

Conversely, think about how much easier it is for your prospect to say no a few days later when they have forgotten your name and saying no is as easy as not returning your phone calls and emails. It's not rocket science, people. Don't get punk'd, and don't punk yourself. Give yourself the best probability for success, and bring the call to a close at the end of your sales presentation. Yes is best, but no is a perfectly acceptable answer.

The third reason you should bring the call to a conclusion is because once it's over, it's over. It's in the past, and I can tell you without equivocation and with total confidence that *only losers live in the past.*

PAST, PRESENT, AND FUTURE

There are three dimensions of time: the past, the present, and the future. (I realize there are some moonbeams out there who will argue there are at least four dimensions of time, but we're going to keep it real pragmatic here.)

One of the most valuable lessons I have learned from really successful people is that the most successful people live in the present moment. Yes, they review the past to learn; yes, they look to the future to plan. *But the vast majority of their time is spent with their consciousness focused on the present moment and on what they can do TODAY to move closer to their desired outcomes in life and business.*

Think about the biggest loser you know. Where does he spend his conscious thoughts? Exactly! *In the past.* Losers are forever angry, bitter, resentful, or hurt about something from their past. They are angry at the ex-wife, or the ex-boss, or the guy who got the promotion over him, or the guy who cut him off in traffic earlier that day, or the guy who impressed the boss at yesterday's meeting. Losers are always hurt or angry over something from the past. When bad things happen, it really sucks. Why in the world would we want to relive things that sucked? Yet, that's what losers do.

On the other hand, there are the insecure neurotics who live their lives worrying about things in the future that will probably never happen. They are worried about someone leaving them in the future or not having enough leads next month or a thousand other irrational fears about the future.

So you've got the losers in the past and the neurotics in the future. Meanwhile, you've got the successful winners living in the present moment and focusing all their energy and effort capitalizing on today's opportunities and responsibilities.

Why? Because that is what winners do.

• • •

So, when the sales opportunity is over, let it float into your past but don't let your consciousness go with it. The likelihood of getting that deal is diminishing with every passing second. We live in a hyper-competitive world with a million distractions. Once you leave your prospect, something else will grab his attention, and someone else will likely build a better relationship and earn his business. Don't delude yourself into thinking otherwise.

None of this means that you shouldn't follow up with your prospects. If your prospect says to call her back next Tuesday, by all means call her back next Tuesday. Just don't call her back with the expectation of her miraculously offering you the money she wouldn't give you following the initial presentation. And if your boss says work your no-sales, by all means work your no-sales. Just don't work them with the expectation that you're going to become a top producer by retilling old ground.

And above all, do not let anything that might happen with your prospect in the future distract you from the sales opportunities that are right in front of you. *Never* squander a lead.

> TO BECOME A TOP PRODUCER, YOU HAVE TO HAVE A STRONG SENSE OF SELF AND BE WILLING TO PERFORM WITH A LITTLE TENSION IN THE AIR.

A primary reason salespeople are reluctant to bring the call to a conclusion is an irrational fear of not being liked by our prospects because we asked them for their business. People may call this a fear of rejection, but I don't think people fear being rejected by strangers. I think people fear not being liked.

Obviously, in sales it's important that prospects like you, because people buy from people they like and trust. However, if you have a *desperate* need to be liked, you'll never ask the tough questions or hold your prospects accountable. You'll also never be a top producer. To become a top producer, you have to have a strong sense of self and be willing to perform with a little tension in the air. Tension and stress are *always* present when we make large purchasing decisions. If you can't cope with a little tension and stress, you're going to have a difficult time closing business.

ANXIETY IS NORMAL

The anxiety people experience when spending money is normal. Don't let it scare you. You have to be willing to deal with the tension, because closing sometimes requires asking tough questions, and tough questions often elevate your prospect's anxiety. It's natural. It's normal. And you have to be willing to deal with it. The bottom line is that in order to be able to close, you have to be self-confident enough that you are not desperate to be liked—and you must get comfortable with the uncomfortable.

I remember a talented young man who used to work for me. I'll call him Fred. He was in his late twenties and had the kind of natural ability to connect with people like I'd never seen. He was handsome and charming, and people warmed up to him within moments of meeting him. People instantly liked and trusted Fred. But Fred couldn't sell a coat in the North Pole to a naked man.

You see, Fred had been a high school and college football star. Everyone loved him and wanted to be his friend. Women wanted him, and men wanted to be him. Fred was the consummate Big Man on Campus. The problem was that Fred fell in love with the adulation, and now he was in the real world where nobody gave a rip about his glory days. But poor Fred still yearned to be loved. In fact, he was desperate for people to like him, and as a result, he was afraid to ask the tough questions necessary to earning a prospect's business.

So despite the fact that Fred could quickly build rapport and earn trust, he became an unpaid consultant. I worked with him for months, but I simply could not get him to give up his desperate need to be liked and to ask the tough questions.

One morning, Fred came into our sales meeting with a grin that went from ear to ear. "Weldon! I got the best lead *ever* last night!"

"Wow!" I responded. "Tell me what happened!" I was genuinely excited for Fred. Maybe he was getting it.

"Well, I went on a lead last night with this older

gentlemen, and we hit it off like two old friends. We talked fishing and hunting for two hours. *I think the guy wants to adopt me!* He is going take me hunting this fall!"

Fred was stoked.

The curiosity was killing me. "So what did he buy from you, Fred?"

"Oh," Fred said sheepishly. "He wasn't ready to buy, but I guarantee you that when he is ready he will call *me*."

"Fred, are you kidding me? I mean the guy called and set the appointment, because he wants a new heating and air-conditioning system. And, you know, we are a heating and air-conditioning company. You know that, right?"

I couldn't imagine how Fred could have the kind of relationship he had with a prospect who needed our product and service and not sell him *something*. I was literally flabbergasted.

"Fred, do me a favor and call him right now," I said.

"Well, uh, he said he's going to call me when he's ready."

"Fred," I continued, "Don't worry. I am not going to have you do anything crazy like ask for his business. Just do me a favor and call him to see if he has any questions."

I figured once Fred got him on the phone and answered a few questions, I could jump on the call and close it. I mean we were less than twelve hours from when Fred left him. Maybe I could save the deal.

Fred made the call and put it on speaker. "Hey, Mr. Prospect, this is Fred. I just wanted to call and see if you had any other questions for me about your heating and air-conditioning system."

To which the gentleman responded, "Oh, which one are you?"

Poor Fred. He lost his job and his new adopted father in the same instant. Don't be desperate for people to like you. Be willing to ask the tough questions. Don't be a Fred. Closing does not mean beating your prospect into submission. If you have extended yourself emotionally and professionally to your prospect and laid all the appropriate groundwork in the early stages of the sales process, closing will be a natural part of the conversation,

It's just like the dynamic of dating. If you rush things at the beginning, you'll scare off your date. But if you take your time, show genuine interest, and focus on building the relationship, there will come a time when there is an expectation of a commitment.

ALWAYS BE CLOSING. NOT.

In the old days of selling, it was about the ABCs—Always Be Closing. (Think *Glengarry Glen Ross*. How can we forget "Coffee is for . . . closers!"?) The basic strategy was to spend 10 percent of your time acting like you were interested in your prospect, and then 90 percent of your time closing, closing, closing.

I prefer to do just the opposite. Invest 90 percent of your time and energy into serving and building the relationship, and you'll find yourself spending only 10 percent of your time and energy closing. This does not mean you can ask for the order only one time and then give up.

Even if your prospect likes you, even if your prospect loves your company, even if your prospect wants and needs your product and service, even if your prospect thinks the price is fair and that your offer has tremendous value, he would still prefer to postpone spending his money. It's in his and everyone else's DNA. Even though closing is less conflicted if you have done your job up front, you may still need to ask for the order a few times.

Stay focused on the process of selling and not getting too emotionally invested in the outcome of closing. Your job is to diagnose and recommend. Your prospect's job is to buy or not buy. Diagnosing and recommending is the process. Buying or not buying is the outcome. To succeed in sales, it is critical to stay focused on the process.

You can't focus on creating one thing and accidentally create something else. I believe this statement with all my heart. This does not mean, however, that there will not be short-term setbacks (such as the occasional no). What it means is that ultimately your long-term outcome will be a reflection of your process. Your short-term outcomes are generally out of your control.

YOU HAVE A CHOICE

As I stated earlier, the sales profession can be broken down into the process and the result, and sales professionals have a choice (as we all do) whether to focus their time and energy on building relationships and trust and solving problems (the process of sales) or focus their time and energy on how much commission they will earn if they make a sale (the outcome of sales).

In sales, you have 100 percent control over the process (which involves your willingness and ability to extend yourself emotionally and professionally to your clients) and zero percent control over whether or not the client writes a check. Of course, you can influence the client's decision, and there is a corresponding relationship between how well you execute your sales process and how often clients say yes. But at the end of the day, the client decides whether or not he is going to write the check.

If you want to successfully manage your life and business, focus on the process. You are in total control of how well you perform the process, so focus on that. Don't focus exclusively on the outcome, which you can't control.

Here is a great example: On January 16, 2010, on the road to an eventual Super Bowl victory, the head coach of my beloved New Orleans Saints, Sean Payton, inspired his team before a key play-off game by presenting them with baseball bats inscribed with the words "Bring the Wood." Coach Payton, who demonstrated enormous character by taking over the Saints in post-Katrina New Orleans, inspired his players to perform at their very best. It worked, and the Saints routed the Arizona Cardinals.

Coach Payton didn't tell his team they had to win (although he was probably thinking, "You BETTER WIN!"). Instead, he told them to perform at their very best. He knew he had the better team. If they performed at their best (the process), he knew they would get the win (the outcome).

I believe as long as we "bring the wood" in our sales career we will eventually rendezvous with wealth, success, and prosperity. It's just a matter of time. Bringing the wood in your sales career is all about serving your prospects by extending yourself emotionally and professionally and focusing on what you can control—the process.

CLOSING THE OPPORTUNITY

Everything you have done on the sales call to this point puts you in a great position to close the opportunity. Bringing the wood really comes down to *asking for the order and closing the sales opportunity*. At this point in the sales process, you have been a great presenter, but you don't get paid for presenting. You get paid for closing.

Power Question #7 is asking for the order! My first ask is always my signature close—"Will you trust me?"

The funny thing about sales is that you get paid for the last few minutes of the sales call. In fact, your income, where your kids go to school, where you go on vacation, when you retire, and how much money you retire with all depend on what you do in the last few minutes of the sales call. But if you have followed the process and closed the doors in the sales hallway, you are uniquely prepared to close the opportunity and earn the prospect's business.

The key to closing is to specifically ask for the order and politely and respectfully hold your prospect accountable to everything he has said and agreed to as you escorted him down the sales hallway. You must have the courage and confidence to hold your prospect accountable to his previous public declarations.

I believe it is critical to have a prepared and rehearsed "closing sequence." Having a closing sequence can make the closing process less stressful while also improving your closing effectiveness.

If there is ever a time where a sales professional tenses up, it's at the end of the presentation as the conversation turns to money and commitment. Let's face it: *Everyone* gets tense when it comes to making a commitment and spending money, including your prospect. Having a clear, precise plan to follow when closing can help keep you on track as the natural tension grows between you and your prospect.

As you approach the close, the prospect often shifts the focus and sometimes introduces red herrings to avoid making a decision. Often these issues can knock you off your beam and shift your focus, thereby causing you to lose control of the entire process at a critical time.

Thus, having a specific closing sequence—knowing exactly what you are going to say and what questions you are going to ask—can help maintain your focus and keep the process moving toward the ultimate goal of closing the opportunity and earning a commission.

I prefer keeping my close simple, honest, and direct. If I have genuinely extended myself to my prospect on an emotional and professional level, created an appropriate solution to their problem, and offered a fair value, I feel I have earned the right to ask for the order.

If you have planned and rehearsed your closing sequence, you will be able to march straight down your path with confidence and certainty. Your prospect will sense that confidence and be inclined to trust you.

BE THE EXPERT, AND MAKE SPECIFIC RECOMMENDATIONS

To successfully close, you must make specific recommendations to the prospect's problems and have legitimate reasons for making the recommendation. I believe it is mandatory that any recommendation you make must be appropriate.

I realize that a common sales practice is to show the prospect several options and then ask, "What makes sense to you?" or "Which of these options is best for you?" Nevertheless, I find it far more compelling to recommend a solution based on your expertise and everything you have learned about your prospect's problems. You are the expert and are supposed to know what the best solution is.

How would you feel if you went to your doctor and your doctor said, "Jeez, Santiago. You have some pretty serious health problems here. What do you suppose we should do?" I don't know about you, but I expect my doctor to recommend an appropriate solution. She is the expert. It is her job to know.

I believe it's the same for sales professionals. We are the experts. It's our responsibility to know what the prospect needs to solve his problem, and we should have a specific and simple recommendation. Remember: The confused mind says, "NO!"

Here is a real-life example that illustrates how the expert should solve a problem.

A couple years ago, I went in for a physical. During the examination, my doctor found something suspicious in my neck.

"Um," he said, "We've got something here."

"I know. You've got my neck." I shot back.

"Yeah, I know that, wise guy. But I feel something else. I am going to send you for a test."

A few weeks later, I was lying in a dark examination room having an ultrasound on my neck. All I could see was the guy's face doing the exam and two computer screens up on the wall.

"Um," he mumbled as he clicked around on his keyboard.

"What do you mean, *Um?*"

"Oh, I'm not sure. Probably nothing. Your doctor will discuss the results with you."

A few days later, I was back with the original doctor, feeling a little frustrated by all the ambiguity.

"Well," he began, "We aren't sure what we've got here. I am going to send you to another doctor for another test."

"Really?" I asked, "Another doctor and another test? What the hell is going on?"

"I am not sure. Probably nothing to worry about. But I'd rather be safe than sorry."

At this point, I wasn't worried, but I was more than a little confused and aggravated.

A week or two later, I arrived at a third doctor's office. As you know, I am no rocket scientist, but even a knucklehead like me starts putting two and two together when I realized my third doctor was an oncologist. Now, I was worried.

The third doctor did about twenty small biopsies called fine needle biopsies to check my thyroid for cancer. He called me a few days later.

"Well, we got the results back and they are inconclusive. There is a 50/50 shot that you have thyroid cancer."

"A 50/50 shot?" I asked. "That's the best you can do?"

"Unfortunately, yes. I am sending you to another doctor. He'll have some options for you to consider."

At this point I was nervous, worried, and confused. I made the mistake of using the Internet to get more information, which only made me more nervous, worried, and confused. While the Internet is great for email, beyond that it is a tool of the devil. If you've ever lost a sale because the Internet confused your prospect, you know what I mean.

A couple of weeks later, I was sitting in the fourth doctor's office.

"Looks like there is a 50/50 chance you've got thyroid cancer."

"So I've heard," I responded. "Anything more you can tell me?"

"Well, you've got a few options. You can ignore it, as relatively few people die from thyroid cancer. Or we can do surgery to remove half of your thyroid. While you are on the operating table, I'll have it taken upstairs to do a definitive cancer test. If it's cancer, I'll take out the other half. If it's not cancer, I'll sew you up with half a thyroid."

"What are the risks?" I asked.

"Well, sometimes we are wrong. I could sew you up with half a thyroid, and we could find out later the cancer is back. The real risk is the surgery itself. We get real close to your vocal chords. There is a small chance I could nick something, and you could lose your voice—permanently. There is a pretty good chance you'll have some voice and hoarseness issues even if everything goes perfectly."

"So two potential surgeries mean twice the odds of vocal issues?" I wondered aloud.

"Exactly."

"I make my living as a professional speaker. No speaking, no income," I responded.

Then, he said the words I had longed to hear.

"Mr. Long, here is what I am going to recommend, and here is why. I suggest we do one surgery to minimize the risk of voice issues. During that surgery, I'll remove your entire thyroid. If it turns out to be cancer, we'll have the whole thing. If it turns out not to be cancer, well, better safe than sorry, right? Either way I'll give you a little pill to replace what your thyroid normally does. You'll be good as new before you know it."

When he finished, I felt more at ease than I had in months. Finally, someone knew what to do. Finally, someone was in control. Finally, I didn't feel confused and overwhelmed.

A few weeks later I had my thyroid removed and learned that I did, indeed, have thyroid cancer. I was happy to have it out of my body, as I would have been none too excited about sharing my body with cancer. I am a little selfish that way.

The moral of the story is this: Sometimes your prospects are confused, worried, and a little overwhelmed. Take control of the situation, and make it simple for them. Demonstrate that you are an expert and know exactly what to do. Tell them exactly what you are going to recommend, why you are making the recommendation, and ask for the damn order!

You are the expert, and if you've done your job correctly, you should know exactly what your prospect needs.

WILL YOU TRUST ME? (POWER QUESTION #7)

Let's take a look at a closing sequence. I'll use financial services as an example, but you should be able to easily insert your specific information. The closing sequence includes the following points:

1. Explaining the available solutions
2. Recommending the appropriate solution
3. Explaining the recommendation
4. Reminding the prospect about the emotions he will experience by making this purchase and your guarantee of service and satisfaction
5. Asking for the order (Will you trust me?)

From the point of asking for the order for the first time, you will see how easy it is to overcome any and all objections by holding your prospect accountable to what he previously said and agreed to. Keep in mind you may need to ask for the order a few times, but you will see just how easy that is if you've closed all the doors in the sales hallway.

All it takes is preparation, courage, and confidence.

Let's go back to the example of selling financial services. Keep in mind that although your prospect was originally only concerned about getting a new car, during the questioning process he asked us to consider college tuition for his kid when designing a solution.

> *Sales Professional:* "Mr. Prospect, I'd like to share a few options with you that will ensure that you have adequate savings to get that Land Rover. First of all, this is plan ABC (explain option ABC). Another option for you is plan XYZ (explain option XYZ).
>
> Now, I am going to recommend option ABC, and here is why (explain exactly why ABC is the best option).
>
> For your son's tuition needs you have a couple of options. First of all, there is option DEF (explain option DEF). Another way to go is option LMN (explain option LMN).
>
> Based on what you told me earlier, I am going to recommend option LMN, and here is why (explain why option LMN is perfectly tailored to his situation).
>
> Now, Mr. Prospect, I realize there are a hundred different companies that could take care of your financial planning, but if you trust me and my company, I can promise you several things. First of all, with this plan you'll definitely have the money to get that four-wheel-drive Land Rover, which is going to give you that feeling of safety (the emotion driving the purchasing decision) on snowy days. Second, if you trust me with this plan, you will have tuition money for your son that guarantees him a college education and will make you feel like Dad of the Year (the emotion driving the purchasing decision).

And third, if any of these things don't happen and you are unhappy for any reason, I give you my word that I'll move heaven and earth to make things right.

So the only question I have for you now is simple: *Will you trust me with this recommendation?*"

At this point, simply wait as long as it takes for the prospect to respond. Get comfortable with the silence. And do not become disappointed if he raises some objections at this point. Remember human nature? You should *expect* some resistance at this point. This is where you go to work. Everything you have done up to this point has prepared you for what comes next.

You are ready to hold your prospect accountable.

OVERCOMING OBJECTIONS

When the prospect brings up any objections and maybe even some stall tactics, you simply must use the three most powerful words in sales: "Earlier you said . . . "

Prospect: "Well, yeah, I mean, I trust you. I'm just not sure I can save that much every month." (money objection)

Sales Professional: "I see. Well, earlier you said that you needed $5000 for the Land Rover down payment, which works out to three dollars a day over the next five years, which you agreed was less than a Starbucks a day. Has that changed over the course of our discussion?"

Prospect: "Well, no. I guess not."

Sales Professional: "Great. Let's go ahead and write up the paperwork."

Prospect: "Well, um. How about this: I am probably going to do this. It makes sense. But what I'd like to do is put some pencil to paper, and make sure it's all going to work. But I'm definitely going to do it. How about I call you on Tuesday, and we'll meet up and do the paperwork?" (The "I want to think about it" objection).

Sales Professional: "Well, it's up to you, but I am a little confused. Earlier you said that once I answered all your questions, designed the right plan, and got it within your budget, you'd let me know one way or the other whether it's a good fit for your family. Now, it sounds like you are not sure. Has anything changed?"

Prospect: "No, no. Nothing has changed. I think it's a good plan. I just need to put pencil to paper, you know?"

Sales Professional: "I understand it's a big decision, but since nothing has changed, how about I go ahead and start the paperwork?"

At this point we could go on forever if I have adequately addressed all the issues as we walked down the sales hallway. Imagine the bind I would be in if the three dollars a day had not already been addressed. I could raise it at the end, but I could not refer the prospect back to what he said and agreed to.

There is a gigantic difference between *me* telling him it's only one cup of coffee per day and *referring him back to when he said it*. Don't forget: Only *his* public declarations dictate *his* future actions. *My* public declarations are likely to have no affect on his future actions.

It is very important to understand during the close that your prospect may never say yes. It is also very important to understand that no is a perfectly acceptable answer. If I get the feeling after a few times of asking for the order that the answer is going to be no, I will take that for an answer. What I am not going to do is get punk'd into crossing my fingers and placing all my hope on next Tuesday.

If I have asked for the order several times and reminded the prospect about what he previously said and agreed to, and he doesn't say "yes," I will eventually say something like this:

> *Sales Professional*: "Mr. Prospect, earlier you said if I answered all your questions, designed the perfect plan, and got it within the budget, you'd let me know one way or the other whether I am a good fit for you and your family. Do you believe I haven't done those things, or are you looking for a polite way to say no? Keep in mind that no is a perfectly acceptable answer."

If my prospect says no at that point, I will respectfully

and politely thank him for his time and the opportunity to serve and move on. I don't take it personally. I don't get hurt.

If my prospect at that point says, "No, no. I am not saying no. I'm just not sure," I will hang in there and keep asking until I get a definitive yes or no. Remember, if I can get my prospect to make a definitive decision with me in front of him, I've got a much higher probability of that decision being a yes.

> AND IT'S REALLY IN EVERYONE'S
> BEST INTEREST TO GET THE
> SITUATION RESOLVED—
> FOR BETTER OR FOR WORSE.

As you know, I am not saying it will always be straightforward, and I am not saying there won't be times where your prospect has a bona fide reason to wait until Tuesday. I am just saying that unless you are selling some superduper complicated nuclear waste disposal system, people can usually make a decision if they want to. And even if your sales process is long and convoluted, there comes a time where push comes to shove. And it's really in everyone's best interest to get the situation resolved—for better or for worse.

Let's take an example from the contracting service industry, where price is always an issue. I'll use a technique called "dollarizing the value" or, as some call it, "reduce it to the ridiculous" combined with "earlier you said . . . "

We'll assume I've already made my recommendation and explained why it's the appropriate solution.

> *Sales Professional*: "Mr. Prospect, I realize that there are fifty companies you could have in your home to do this project. What I can promise you is this: If you trust me and my company, I guarantee that everything will go exactly as I've promised. And if it doesn't, I give you my word that I'll personally move heaven and earth to fix it. So the only question I have for you is simple: Will you trust me with this project?"

> *Prospect*: "Well, I don't know. You are a thousand bucks higher than the other guy."

> *Sales Professional*: "I see. You know, Mr. Prospect, *earlier you said* that companies try to save time and money by cutting steps on the installation. Do you think the other guy might be doing that?"

> *Prospect*: "I'm not sure. He seemed like a good guy."

> *Sales Professional*: "I am sure he is. Let me ask you this: Suppose the other guy and I offered you the exact same price. Who would you go with then?"

> *Prospect*: "Well, you, of course."

> *Sales Professional*: "So you agree there is value in my company. You just aren't sure if that value is worth the extra thousand dollars."

Prospect: "Exactly."

Sales Professional: "Mr. Prospect, do you realize that over the twenty-year life of this installation, that works out to one dollar per week? Do my company, the service, and the guarantees seem like they're worth one dollar per week?"

Prospect: "Yeah. I guess."

Sales Professional: "I agree. With your permission, I'll get the paperwork started."

Suppose, even after all you've done, your prospect still wants to get competitive proposals.

Prospect: "I just don't know. Maybe I should talk to another company."

Sales Professional: "Mr. Prospect, earlier you said that if you had to choose between multiple companies who might tell you anything to get their hands on your money or one company who would treat you the way we treated Mrs. Jones, you would choose the company that would treat you like Mrs. Jones. Has that changed over the last ninety minutes?"

Prospect: "Not really."

Sales Professional: "How about I go ahead and get the paperwork started?"

The bottom line is that if you have a reputable company, great quality, service, and a fair price, there is really no reason to say no. All you have to do is remind them of what they said and agreed to and keep asking for the business in a respectful and polite tone.

Eventually you will resolve the issue with a yes or no.

Closing the sales opportunity does not have to be stressful and chaotic. It can be a respectful and casual conversation. Just remember that humans are inclined to postpone spending their money. With preparation and the courage and confidence to hold your prospect accountable, you will find yourself increasingly closing more business.

If you have properly prepared for closing the sales opportunity, you will have the ability to politely and respectfully hold your prospect accountable to what he previously told you. Nevertheless, you will likely need to ask several times.

The bottom line is really very simple: After you ask for the order the first time with "Will you trust me?" see what your prospect says.

If she says yes, she'll be signing something.

If she says no, it will be for one of three reasons: Price; I need more bids; or I want to think about it, which can be disguised in a million different ways. But if it's not a price or "I need more bids" objection, everything else is basically "I want to think about it."

If it's a three-bid objection, simply remind your prospect about your previous conversation: "Mr. Prospect, earlier you said that you preferred my company over getting three bids from companies who might say anything to get your money. Has that changed over our time together?"

Prospect: "No."

You: "Great. Let's go ahead and start the paperwork!"

If it's a price objection, simply remind your prospect about your previous conversation: "Mr. Prospect, earlier you said that price was not the most important consideration. Has that changed?"

Prospect: "Well, not really. But it's a lot of money."

You: "I understand it's a big decision, but with your permission let's start the paperwork."

If it's not one of those objections, simply treat it as an "I want to think about it" objection. Regardless of the excuse, remind your prospect of their conversation earlier at the intention statement.

You: "Will you trust me with this recommendation?"

Prospect: "Well, I trust you, but we always think about these things overnight."

You: "I understand it's a big decision, but earlier you said you could let me know today whether or not we are a good fit. And of course 'no' is a perfectly acceptable answer. Has that changed over our time together?"

Prospect: "Not really. I just always like to think (pray, sleep, talk to my priest, take my dog to the vet, talk to my banker, etc.) about these things."

You: "I get it. But with your permission I'd like to go ahead and start the paperwork."

You have to understand that when you hold your prospect accountable to his previous declarations, it's very natural for him to feel some anxiety, because *he did make those public declarations!*

So it's normal for him to say anything out of nervous energy. When he stops talking, simply throw him a life preserver by asking for the order again. *Don't take the bait when he brings up some crazy excuse!* Just acknowledge it and ask for the order again.

Once you hold him accountable to his previous public declarations a few times, one of two things is going to happen: He'll either say yes or no, and no is a perfectly acceptable answer!

Whatever the prospect's final decision, you will be free to move on to new opportunities. Using the principle of consistency, however, will give you the highest probability for success, as your prospect will be inclined to act in a manner consistent with the public declarations he made to you.

CONCLUSION

Consistency in sales is the objective. Consistency in the process is the way to get there. Consistent sales activities produce consistent results.

Yet consistency is two-fold. On one hand, it means that we follow a consistent process to get consistent results. On the other hand, the Consistency Principle helps us leverage the reality that public declarations dictate future actions.

Focus on what you control (the process)—not what someone else controls (the result). Stay focused on the process over which you have 100 percent control. Be the very best you can be, and let the chips fall where they may. Focus on executing your professional responsibilities—not stressing about the outcome—and closing can be as natural as a friendly conversation.

Ask questions that prompt your prospects to make public declarations consistent with what you want them to do at the end of the process—purchase from you.

I realize it's difficult to try something new. You will ask yourself, "Can I do it? Is it worth the effort?"

But when you ask those questions, ask yourself another question: "How bad do you want it?"

The reality is you CAN do this, and it IS worth the effort. And the good news is that leveraging Consistency Selling and running your sales calls the way you should is easy. The bad news is it will always be a little easier to drop off a price and hope the prospect calls you next Tuesday. Problem is, Tuesday never comes, does it?

The combination of consistency in your actions and the effect of the prospect's public declarations can bring new levels of success in your sales career. It can change your income. It can change your zip code. And you'll have fat, happy little children.

Happy selling, my friend.

INDEX

ABOUT THE AUTHOR

Weldon Long is a successful entrepreneur, sales expert, and author of *The Power of Consistency*, a *New York Times* bestseller, and *The Upside of Fear*. In 2009, his business was selected by *Inc.* magazine as one of America's fastest growing privately held companies.

Weldon is one of the nation's most powerful speakers and a driven motivator who teaches the Sales and Prosperity Mindset philosophies that catapulted him from desperation and poverty to a life of wealth and prosperity.

Weldon is honored to have served some of America's finest companies, including Comcast, The Franklin Covey Organization, The Home Depot, FedEx, Tom Hopkins International, Wells Fargo Bank, Owens Corning, and Farmers Insurance.

Mr. Long lives in Colorado with his wife, Taryn, and their children, Hunter and Skylar.

For more information, visit www.WeldonLong.com.

VISIT **WWW.CONSISTENCYSELLING.COM** AND GET **FREE** INSTANT ACCESS TO THREE POWERFUL VIDEOS THAT WILL HELP YOU **IMMEDIATELY** IMPLEMENT THE PROSPERITY MINDSET AND CONSISTENCY SELLING.